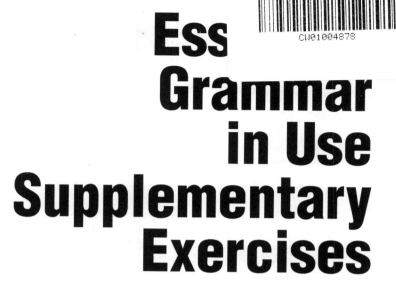

Essential Grammar in Use Supplementary Exercises

Helen Naylor
with Raymond Murphy

CAMBRIDGE
UNIVERSITY PRESS

Published by the Press Syndicate of the University of Cambridge
The Pitt Building, Trumpington Street, Cambridge CB2 1RP
40 West 20th Street, New York, NY 10011–4211, USA
10 Stamford Road, Oakleigh, Melbourne 3166, Australia

© Cambridge University Press 1996

First published 1996

Printed in Great Britain
by Scotprint Ltd., Musselburgh, Scotland

A catalogue record for this book is available from the British Library.

ISBN 0 521 46998 8 Supplementary Exercises (without answers)
ISBN 0 521 46997 X Supplementary Exercises (with answers)
ISBN 0 521 55927 8 Essential Grammar in Use (without answers)
ISBN 0 521 55928 6 Essential Grammar in Use (with answers)

Contents

To the teacher
Thanks

To the teacher

Essential Grammar in Use Supplementary Exercises offers extra practice of most of the grammar covered in *Essential Grammar in Use*. Much of the language is contextualised within dialogues, letters, articles, etc., encouraging students to consider meaning as well as form. The book can be used as self-study material or as a basis for further practice in class or as homework.
It is designed for students who have already worked through the exercises in *Essential Grammar in Use* (or elsewhere), but who need more, or more challenging, practice. It is particularly useful for revision work.

The exercises are organised in the same order as the units of *Essential Grammar in Use*, and the numbers of the relevant *Essential Grammar in Use* units are shown in the top right-hand corner of each page. Although the grammar areas are not covered in order of difficulty in the book as a whole, there is a progression where several exercises are offered on one area. For example, Exercise 7 requires students to use given verbs in the correct form, Exercise 8 requires them to write complete positive and negative sentences and Exercise 9 requires them to write complete questions within the context of a conversation. The contextualised practice in the book offers the opportunity for much further practice, using the exercises as models or springboards for speaking and writing practice of a freer nature. The symbol ☺ is used where a student is required to write freely from personal experience.

Thanks

For trying out exercises, and offering valuable comments: The English Department, Al Azhar University, Cairo, Egypt; The British Council, Athens, Greece; International House, Lódź, Poland; The British Council, Bologna, Italy; Instituto Español de Bachillerato, Aixovall, Andorra; Gabriela Brunner, Fernando García Clemente, Cemile Iskenderoğlu, Dr Felicity O'Dell, Lelio Pallini, Dr Ramzy Radwan.

I would also like to thank Nóirín Burke and Jeanne McCarten at Cambridge University Press for their help and support. Illustrated by Amanda MacPhail, Mark Peppé and Bill Piggins. Layout by Newton Harris. Edited by Geraldine Mark.

am/is/are

1 Complete the sentences. Use the words in the box.

am ('m)	is ('s)	are ('re)
am not ('m not)	is not (isn't)	are not (aren't)

1 David's new bicycle ...is......... blue.
2 A: Are these your books?
   B: No, they .aren't....
3 My children .... 8 and 6 years old.
4 I .... interested in baseball. I think it's boring.
5 We can walk to the supermarket. It .... far.
6 A: Are you a teacher?
   B: Yes, I ....
7 A: .... those birds from South America?
   B: The red one ...., but the blue one ....
8 When .... your birthday?
9 Kate and Sandra .... at work today because it is a holiday.
10 You .... wrong. 9 x 9 is 81, not 82.
11 .... this is the right bus for the city centre?
12 A: Where .... my shoes?
    B: In your bedroom.

2 Complete the sentences. Use one of the question forms in the box + **is** or **are**.

Where	Who	What
How	Why	How much
What colour	How old	

1 A: *Where are*......... my keys?   B: On the table.
2 A: .... the time, please?   B: Half past five.
3 A: .... your headache now?   B: Much better, thank you.
4 A: .... the holiday photographs? B: In your handbag.
5 A: .... that clock?   B: Three hundred years old.
6 A: .... your new shoes?   B: Red.
7 A: .... Simon happy today?   B: Because it's his birthday.
8 A: .... Maria from?   B: Spain, I think.
9 A: .... these trousers?   B: They're £40.
10 A: .... that man in the car?   B: My uncle.
11 A: .... the banks closed today? B: Because it's a holiday.

3 Write positive or negative sentences. Begin in Box A and choose an ending from Box B.

A		B
1 ~~Peter's parents~~		at work this week. I'm on holiday.
2 The Andes		the capital of the USA.
3 New York		a hot country.
4 Football	am/am not	good for you.
5 Paul	is/isn't	very high mountains.
6 Britain	are/aren't	British. She's American.
7 All the shops		~~on holiday.~~
8 I		closed at lunchtime.
9 Too many chocolates		21 years old today.
10 Sally's teacher		a popular sport in Britain.

1 *Peter's parents are on holiday.*
2 The Andes ....
3 New York ....
4 ....
5 ....
6 ....
7 ....
8 ....
9 ....
10 ....

4 Look at the picture of a family group, and ask questions about the people. Read the answers to the questions first.

YOU: (1) *Who's that man?*
MARIA: That's my father. He's a dentist.
YOU: (2) ....?
MARIA: He's 45.
YOU: (3) .... that .... mother?
MARIA: Yes, it is. She's a dentist, too.
YOU: (4) ....?
MARIA: That's my sister, Laura.
YOU: (5) ....?
MARIA: She's 23.
YOU: (6) .... your brother?
MARIA: No, it's Laura's husband.
YOU: (7) ....?
MARIA: Ferdinand.
YOU: (8) .... those .... grandparents?
MARIA: Yes, they are. That's my mother's father and my father's mother!

5　Use the words in the box below to write sentences. Some of your sentences must be questions (**Where is …?**, **Are your parents …?**, etc.). Use each word at least once.

18	is/isn't	your parents	expensive
I			an engineer
	Jim's book	am/am not	
old		Anna	at work
	Spanish		how
		where	are/aren't

1　Anna isn't Spanish.
2　Where is Jim's book?
3 ....
4 ....
5 ....
6 ....
7 ....
8 ....
9 ....
10 ....

I am doing (present continuous)　　　　**Units 3–4, Appendix 4**

6　How do you spell it? Write these verbs in the continuous form (**-ing**) in the correct list.

~~help~~	~~put~~	~~decide~~	~~die~~	swim	listen	have	forget	write
arrive	play	begin	start	come	stop	win	work	laugh
live	lie	wear	tie	cry	dance	dig	make	rob

+ -ing
helping
....
....
....
....
....
....

t → tt, p → pp, *etc.*
putting
....
....
....
....
....
....

e → ing
deciding
....
....
....
....
....
....

ie → ying
dying
....
....

7 Complete the text about Jane and Mary who are in their office. Use the present continuous (**is/are** + **-ing**) of the verbs in the box. Sometimes the verb is negative (**isn't/aren't** + **-ing**).

write	drink	~~read~~	work	ring	listen	have
think	make	sing	ask	talk	stand	sit

10.30 a.m. Jane is in her office. She (1) _is reading_ some letters and (2) .... her replies. Her secretary, Mary, (3) .... some coffee. She (4) .... a song.

10.40 a.m. Jane and Mary (5) .... their coffee. Jane (6) .... about her holiday plans, but Mary (7) .... to her. She (8) .... about her new car. They (9) .... at the moment; they (10) .... their coffee break.

10.50 a.m. The telephone (11) .... and that is the end of their break. Now it's back to work.

10.55 a.m. Jane (12) .... at her desk. She (13) .... next to the window and (14) .... some questions to an important customer.

8 Look at the picture and the description. Re-write the description to make it correct.

STEVE   FRED   PAM   SAM   ERIC   JO

Steve is reading a newspaper. The children, Sam and Eric, are playing with a ball. They are both wearing sunglasses. Pam is cooking chicken. She's laughing because the smoke is getting in her eyes. Jo is standing with her mother and is listening to music on her personal stereo. She is eating an orange. Fred, the dog, is lying on the grass asleep.

1 Steve _isn't reading the newspaper. He's reading a book._
2 Sam and Eric ....
3 ....
4 ....
5 ....
6 ....
7 ....
8 ....

9   You can hear your mother talking to your grandfather on the telephone. Write the questions your grandfather is asking, using the present continuous (**is/are** + **-ing**). Look at all the answers first.

GRANDFATHER: (1) ....*Are*.... the children ...*watching TV?*....

MOTHER: No, they're in bed.

GRANDFATHER: (2) .... reading?

MOTHER: No, they aren't. They're asleep.

GRANDFATHER: (3) .... Simon ....?

MOTHER: He's writing a postcard and watching TV at the same time.

GRANDFATHER: (4) ....?

MOTHER: A travel programme about India.

GRANDFATHER: (5) .... Anna ....?

MOTHER: No, she isn't watching it. She's in the kitchen, cooking the dinner.

GRANDFATHER: (6) ....?

MOTHER: Lying on the floor and talking to you!

I do/work/like etc. (present simple)   Units 5–7

10   Which of the underlined verbs is right? The information is about the USA.

1   Most shops usually open/~~opens~~ at 8.30 a.m. and close/~~closes~~ at 6.00 p.m.
2   The banks doesn't/don't usually close at lunchtime.
3   Many children has/have a computer at home.
4   The New York subway usually works/work very well.
5   It doesn't/don't often snow in California.
6   Most people don't/doesn't work on Sundays.
7   The capital city, Washington, have/has a population of about one million.
8   Many people in Los Angeles speak/speaks Spanish.
9   Schoolchildren don't/doesn't usually wear uniform.

11   Complete the sentences using the verbs below each picture. Put the verbs into the present simple. For the last sentence for each picture put the verb into the negative.

1 **A lion**

run/eat/have/sleep

It .*has*... a tail.
It .*runs*... very fast.
It .*sleeps*... a lot.
It .*doesn't eat*... fish.

3 **The Sahara Desert**

shine/rain/fall/live

The sun .... every day.
Not many people .... there.
The temperature .... at night.
It .... very much.

2 **Marc, aged 6 months**

read/cry/live/drink

He .... with his Mum and Dad.
He .... orange juice.
He .... a lot.
He .... books.

4 **Birds**

eat/have/like/fly

They .... wings.
They .... insects.
They .... long distances.
They .... cats.

12   Ten sentences are wrong and two sentences are right. Correct the mistakes where necessary.

1   David never take the bus to work. *David never takes the bus to work.*
2   Go you to the office every day? ....
3   My car don't work when it is cold. ....
4   What time the film starts? ....
5   Ben's sister don't speak French but Ben do. ....
6   How many eggs you want for breakfast? ....
7   Does the 9.30 train stop at every station? ....
8   What does do your father? ....
9   I not write many letters. I usually use the telephone. ....
10 What Sue usually have for lunch? ....
11 How much do these apples cost? ....
12 Charlie plays basketball but he doesn't enjoys it. ....

13   First, read and complete the text with phrases from the box.

wakes the children up	10 p.m.	~~a nurse~~	bus
20 children	6 o'clock	many times	St John's Hospital
gives them breakfast	very tired	taxi	

My name is Jennie. I'm (1) *a nurse* and I work at (2) .... I look after sick
children at night. I start work at (3) .... and finish early at (4) .... in
the morning. I go to work by (5) .... but I come home in the morning by
(6) .... because I'm tired. I have (7) .... in my section. I look at the
children (8) .... during the night. Sometimes I sit and talk to a child. The children
sleep most of the time. At 6 o'clock the day nurse arrives and (9) .... She
(10) .... at 7 o'clock. I go home and go to bed at 8 o'clock. I usually feel
(11) ....

Now use this information to complete the questions that John asks Jennie.

12   *What do you do?*
13   Where ....?
14   What time ....?
15   What time ....?
16   How ....?
17   How ....?
18   How many ....?
19   How often ....?
20   When ....?
21   What .... at 7 o'clock?
22   How .... when you go home?

14   Paula is in the city centre. She is asking a woman some questions about her visits to the local cinema. First, read the answers that the woman gives. Then, write the questions that Paula asks.

PAULA: (1) *How often do you go to the cinema?*
WOMAN: Usually once a week.
PAULA: (2) .... alone?
WOMAN: No, with a friend.
PAULA: (3) .... there?
WOMAN: I walk because I live nearby.
PAULA: (4) ....?
WOMAN: £4.00.
PAULA: (5) ....?
WOMAN: At the back of the cinema.
PAULA: (6) ....?
WOMAN: All kinds of films, especially comedies.
PAULA: (7) .... film?
WOMAN: My favourite is 'Silent Streets'.
PAULA: (8) .... anything, for example, ice-cream?
WOMAN: No, I don't, but I usually have a coke.
PAULA: Thank you for answering my questions.
WOMAN: You're welcome.

Now write the woman's answers in a short paragraph.

She usually (9) *goes* to the cinema once a week with a friend. She (10) .... to the cinema because she (11) .... nearby. The ticket (12) .... £4.00 and she (13) .... at the back of the cinema. She (14) .... all kinds of films, especially comedies. Her favourite film (15) .... 'Silent Streets'. She (16) .... anything but she usually (17) .... a coke.

☺   What about you? Do you go to the cinema? Write a short paragraph like the one above:

I ....
....
....
....
....

I am doing and I do (present continuous and present simple)

15 Present continuous or present simple? Complete the sentences choosing the right verb form.

1 _Do you like_ learning English? (Do you like / Are you liking)
2 .... this programme.
   (I'm not understanding / I don't understand)
3 Jim and his father .... They are asleep.
   (aren't watching / don't watch TV)
4 Tony is upstairs in the bathroom. He .... his hair.
   (washes / is washing)
5 Why ....? Are we late? (do we run / are we running)
6 There are some strange noises in the sitting room. What ....?
   (is Tom doing / does Tom do)
7 What time .... every day?
   (does John get up / is John getting up)
8 Fred and I are good dancers but we .... to discos very often.
   (don't go / aren't going)
9 A: .... from Denmark? B: No, I'm Swedish.
   (Are you coming / Do you come)
10 .... in the same hotel in New York.
   (I always stay / I'm always staying)
11 .... in winter in your country? (Does it snow / Is it snowing)
12 Joanna .... the dinner at the moment.
   (isn't cooking / doesn't cook)
   She .... on the phone. (talks / 's talking)

16 Read about what John **does** before breakfast **every day**, and what he **is doing now**.

Every day John gets up at 6.30 a.m. and does some exercises in the garden. Then he has a shower. He gets dressed and listens to the news on the radio. Then he goes downstairs and makes breakfast. At the moment, John is sitting in the kitchen and drinking a cup of tea. He is reading a magazine and thinking about his holiday.

☺ Now, you write a paragraph about yourself. Use some of the verbs below or think of your own ideas.

(a) 4 things you do before breakfast every day.
   (get up / have a shower / clean my teeth / brush my hair / get dressed / do some exercises / go for a run / read / listen etc.)

and

(b) 4 things you're doing now.
   (write / look (at) / drink / eat / read / sit / learn / do / think / hold / wear / work etc.)
   Every day I ....
   At the moment ....

17 Complete the sentences. Put the verbs into the present simple (e.g. **do**) or present continuous (e.g. **I'm doing**), positive or negative.

1 A: Have a chocolate. B: No thank you. I *don't like chocolate.* (like chocolate)
2 A: Let's have lunch in the garden. B: No, we can't. It *'s raining.* (rain)
3 A: What ....? B: Pam? She's a doctor. (do)
4 Tony .... at the moment. He's on holiday. (work)
5 A: Why ....? B: Because I'm happy. (smile)
6 Sandra and her husband are vegetarian. They .... (eat meat)
7 A: What ....? B: A letter from my sister. (read)
8 A: What time ....? B: Me? About 7.00 a.m. usually. (get up)
9 A: Where's Dave? B: He's in the kitchen. He .... (make coffee)
10 A: How ....? B: I usually catch a bus. (go to work)
11 A: I think Shaun and David are asleep. B: Mmm. Turn the TV off. They .... (watch it)
12 John and I want to go to Greece for our holidays, so we .... (learn Greek)

18 Look at the pictures and the verbs. Write two questions for each picture. Use the present continuous for one question and the present simple for the other question.

1 RUTH: Where *are you going?*
   JAMES: To the cinema.
   RUTH: *Do you like the cinema?*
   JAMES: Yes, I do.

(go / like)

2 YOUNG BOY: What ....?
   WOMAN: I'm a photographer.
   YOUNG BOY: ....?
   WOMAN: I'm putting a film in my camera.

(do / do)

3 JEFF: When .... usually ....?
   BRIAN: At 6 o'clock.
   JEFF: Why .... now?
   BRIAN: Because I have a dentist's appointment.

(finish / leave)

4 LUCY: What ....?
  PAUL: Watching TV, I think.
  LUCY: .... TV a lot?
  PAUL: Yes, every night.

(do / watch)

5 SUE: ....?
  TIM: Looking at a new car.
  SUE: ....?
  TIM: £10,000.

(do / cost)

6 BETH: ....?
  ANNE: Because they're late.
  BETH: ....?
  ANNE: At 8.30 a.m.

(run / start)

19 Write questions and your own positive or negative short answers. Use the present simple or the present continuous.

1 you / have / dinner at the moment?
  Are you having dinner at the moment?   _No, I'm not._

2 you / read / a newspaper every day?
  ....? ....

3 it / snow much in your country?
  ....? ....

4 you / usually / do / your homework on a word processor?
  ....? ....

5 you / drink / coffee now?
  ....? ....

6 you / drink coffee for breakfast every day?
  ....? ....

7 you / work / at the moment?
  ....? ....

8 children / eat lunch at school in your country?
  ....? ....

have got

20 Complete the story about Ruth. Put in **has got** (**'s got**), **have got** (**'ve got**), **hasn't got** or **haven't got**.

Ruth is 21. She (1) _has got_ fair hair and blue eyes. She (2) .... two brothers, William and Phillip, but she (3) .... any sisters. Her brothers (4) .... brown hair and brown eyes. One of her brothers, Phillip, is married and (5) .... two children, so she's an aunt. Ruth lives with her parents in an apartment. It (6) .... five rooms but it (7) .... a garden. She (8) .... her own room in the apartment. In it she (9) .... her computer and a TV. She (10) .... a car but her parents (11) .... one because they can't drive.

☺ What about you? What have you got? Look at Ruth's story and then write about yourself.

hair / eyes? ....
brothers / sisters / parents etc.? ....
house / apartment? ....
computer / car / bicycle / a lot of books etc.? ....
....

21 Write questions. Use **have you got**, **has it got …?** etc.

1 MARY: Tim is a good photographer.
  PAT: What kind of camera _has he got?_

2 STUART: I'm rich!
  VAL: How much money ....?

3 TONY: Kate is going to the dentist this afternoon.
  ALICE: .... toothache?

4 DEREK: Jane and Jim are buying a new house.
  PETER: How many rooms ....?

5 DIANA: Tony wants to talk to you.
  ALEX: .... my telephone number?

6 MARTIN: My sister and brother-in-law have been married for six years.
  ROSE: .... any children?

7 HELEN: My neighbours love cats.
  PAM: How many ....?

8 LAURA: My bag is very heavy.
  ADAM: What .... in it?

22 Put in **has got** (**'s got**), (**'ve got**). Use the positive, negative or question forms.

1 Those flowers are really beautiful and they _'ve got_ a wonderful smell.
2 I must write down John's telephone number. .... a pen?
3 Mary works very hard so she .... time for many hobbies.
4 New York .... a very interesting modern art museum.
5 I can't show you the photographs because I .... them with me.
6 Tigers .... strange, yellow eyes.
7 'What kind of Walkman .... Carol ....?' 'A Sony, I think.'

was/were and I worked/got/went etc. (past simple)

23 Complete the sentences. Use **I/she was** etc. or **we/they were** etc.

1 Liz worked very late last night.   *She was* tired.
2 Jack lost his job yesterday.   .... angry.
3 We laughed a lot at last night's film.   .... very funny.
4 Joe and Sam fell into the river yesterday.   .... wet and cold.
5 Yesterday was a beautiful day.   .... sunny.
6 We saw a horror film last Saturday.   .... really frightened.
7 David and Sue didn't have anything to eat yesterday.   .... hungry.
8 I had a wonderful holiday last year.   .... happy.

24 Where were you at these times? Use **I was at/in + a place**.

☺ 1 *I was at the swimming pool* at 6.30 yesterday morning.
2 .... last Saturday.
3 .... at 7 o'clock yesterday evening.
4 .... last Tuesday afternoon.
5 .... at midnight last night.
6 .... at 1 o'clock yesterday.
7 .... ten minutes ago.

25 Write questions with **was/were** + the words in brackets ( ), and give short answers.

1 MAX: My grandmother died in 1976.
   OSCAR: *Was she very old?* (old)
   MAX: No, *she wasn't.*

2 ELSA: James and Ruth had an oral examination yesterday
   BETH: ....? (difficult)
   ELSA: No, ...

3 SALLY: I had a little red sports car in 1993.
   TONY: ....? (fast)
   SALLY: Yes, ...

4 DAVE: Mike got some tickets for the World Cup.
   SUE: ....? (expensive)
   DAVE: No, ...

5 ALAN: I didn't like school when I was young.
   KATE: ....? (lazy)
   ALAN: No, ...

6 BEN: Julia wasn't at work yesterday.
   MARK: ....? (ill)
   BEN: Yes, ...

7 RUTH: My grandfather met the comedians Laurel and Hardy in 1950.
   TOM: ....? (famous)
   RUTH: Yes, ...

12

was/were and I worked/got/went etc. (past simple)

Units 10–12

26   Look at the pictures and complete the sentences in the correct form of the past simple. Use the verb in brackets ( ).

1 _John didn't play football_ yesterday; he _played_ basketball. (play)
2 The museum .... at 9 a.m. last Sunday; it .... at 10 a.m. (open)
3 I .... a glass last night; I .... a plate. (break)
4 We .... to Spain last year; we .... to France. (go)
5 Carol .... fruit for breakfast; she .... an egg. (have)
6 Angus .... trousers for his wedding; he .... a kilt. (wear)

Look at these pictures. Complete the sentences with a past simple verb in the negative.

7 It .... much last winter; it rained a lot.
8 Barbara and Charlie .... last night; they went to the cinema.
9 Tim .... to his parents last week; he telephoned them.
10 We .... to the city centre; we walked.

27 A father asked his child some questions at the end of the day. Write the questions using **Did you ...** with a verb from box A, and choose an ending from box B.

A		B	
~~go~~	have	a big lunch	any money
play	watch	volleyball	your grandmother
have	do	~~school~~	your homework
visit	spend	a history lesson	your favourite TV programme

1 *Did you go to school?*
2 ....?
3 ....?
4 ....?
5 ....?
6 ....?
7 ....?
8 ....?

28 First, complete the story of Maria's day. Choose from the list below. Then, write the questions that you asked Maria.

spaghetti	1 p.m.	the sports centre	9 a.m.	an Italian restaurant	~~8 a.m.~~
half an hour later	my brother	a birthday present	bus	did some work	

I left home at (1) *8 a.m.* yesterday morning and went to college by (2) ....
I arrived there (3) .... My lessons began at (4) ....
and finished at (5) .... I went to (6) .... for
lunch. I met (7) .... there and we had lunch together. We both ate
(8) .... After lunch, I bought (9) .... for
my father, and my brother went to (10) .... to play volleyball. In the
evening I stayed at home and (11) ....

Now complete the questions that you asked Maria.

12 When *did you leave home?*
13 How ....?
14 When ....?
15 What time ....?
16 What time ....?
17 Where ....?
18 Who ....?
19 What ....?
20 What ....?
21 Where ....?
22 What ....?

29 Put in **had**, **didn't have** or **Did ... have?**

1 When I was a student I was always poor. I *didn't have much money.*
2 A: I arrived home very late yesterday. B: .... a lot of work to do at your office?
3 Ann couldn't go to Moscow last week because she .... the correct visa.
4 When my brother and I were children, we .... two dogs and a cat.
5 .... Sue .... a problem with her TV last night?
6 Not many people .... cars in the 1920s.
7 A: The customs officers at Chicago airport stopped my parents when they arrived.
    B: What .... in their suitcases?
    A: Nothing – only their personal things.

30 A postcard from New York. Complete this postcard that Tony received from his friend Helen. Use a verb in the past simple (e.g. **arrived**) or **was/were**. One verb is in the negative.

> Hi Tony!
>
> I'm in San Francisco now. We (1) *arrived* here yesterday. Before that, we
> (2) .... 10 days in New York. It (3) .... wonderful. Pat and I
> (4) .... a lot of interesting places including the Empire State Building. We
> (5) .... to the top – it (6) .... very high, and we
> (7) .... both a bit frightened. We (8) .... a boat along the river to
> see the Statue of Liberty. We (9) .... through Greenwich Village and
> watched many artists at work. The paintings (10) .... expensive so I
> bought one. We also (11) .... to the theatre and saw a new musical – I
> (12) .... it very much. The weather (13) .... OK – a bit wet
> sometimes. But now in San Francisco, it's hot and sunny.
> See you soon.
> Love Helen (and Pat)

☺ Now, you write a postcard to a friend from your last holiday place.

31 Two friends meet after the weekend. Alice had a good weekend but Tim didn't. Write the other half of
the conversation. (Read Alice's answers first.)

TIM: How are you?
ALICE: (1) _(I'm) fine, thanks._
TIM: Did you have a good weekend?
ALICE: (2) ....
TIM: Did you enjoy the film?
ALICE: (3) .... excellent.
TIM: What did you do after that?
ALICE: (4) ....
TIM: That sounds nice. What was the food like?
ALICE: (5) ...., but .... too much! What about you?
        How was your weekend?
TIM: (6) Terrible! .... with the car.
ALICE: Oh dear! I'm sorry to hear that. Are you all right?
TIM: Yes, I'm fine now but I (7) .... a bad headache for two days.
ALICE: And what about the car? Was there a lot of damage?
TIM: It wasn't too bad. The garage (8) .... and I can drive it again now.
ALICE: Oh, well. Come and have some lunch with me and forget about the weekend.

I was doing and I did
(past continuous and past simple)

32 Look at the picture. This was the scene in Rosamund Street at 10.30 a.m. yesterday. Write what was
happening and where it was happening. Use the past continuous.

1 _Felix was sleeping on a car._
2 ....
3 ....
4 ....
5 ....
6 ....

7 ....

8 ....

9 ....

☺ And you? What were you doing yesterday at …? Use the past continuous.

10 10.30 a.m.   At 10.30 a.m. yesterday I ....

11 12.30 p.m.   ....

12 4.00 p.m.   ....

13 8.30 p.m.   ....

14 1.00 a.m.   ....

33 Complete the conversations. Use **was/were**, or use the past simple (**I did**, etc.) or the past continuous (**was doing**, etc.) of the verb in brackets ( ).

1 POLICEMAN: What _were you doing_ (you / do) when the accident _happened_ (happen)?
   COLIN: I _was_ at the bus-stop. I _was waiting_ (wait) for a bus.
   POLICEMAN: .... (you / see) the accident?
   COLIN: No, because I .... (read) the newspaper.

2 NICOLA: I .... (telephone) you at 9 o'clock last night but you were not at home.
   MARTIN: 9 o'clock? I .... (sit) in a café, ... (drink) hot chocolate.
   NICOLA: .... Jane with you?
   MARTIN: No, she .... (work) in the library.
   NICOLA: Where .... (you / go) after the café?
   MARTIN: I .... (go) home.

3 MUM: Oh no! My beautiful new plate. What happened?
   ANGELA: I'm really sorry, Mum. I .... (break) it when I .... (wash) it.
   MUM: How?
   ANGELA: My hands .... wet and I .... (drop) it on the floor.

4 SOPHIE: .... (you / think) yesterday's exam .... difficult?
   EDWARD: No, not really, but I .... (not / write) very much.
   SOPHIE: Why not?
   EDWARD: Because I .... (dream) about my holidays.

5 ANDREW: There .... a crash outside my house yesterday.
   PIPPA: What .... (happen)?
   ANDREW: I don't know. It .... (rain) but the drivers .... (not / go) fast.
   PIPPA: Were they hurt?
   ANDREW: One man .... (break) his arm and the other man .... (cut) his head.

6 TRACY: Pardon? I didn't hear you. Could you repeat that, please?
   NEIL: I .... (not / talk) to you.
   TRACY: Who .... (you / talk) to?
   NEIL: Sarah.
   TRACY: Oh, sorry.

34 At 10.05 a.m. yesterday, there was a robbery at the Midwest Bank. You are a police officer and you are asking a man some questions about what he was doing, what other people were doing, and what he saw. Write the questions. Use **was/were**, the past simple (**did you …**) and the past continuous (**were you …**).

'Now then, Mr Smith, I know you saw the robbery yesterday. I would like to ask you to some questions. First of all, …

1 What / you / do / at 10.05 a.m. yesterday?
   What were you doing at 10.05 a.m. yesterday?
2 Where / be / Joan Turner? ....?
3 What / Mrs Jones / do? ....?
4 Where / Mrs Walters / go? ....?
5 How many robbers / go / into the bank?
   ....?
6 they / carry / guns? ....?
7 Where / the big car / wait? ....?
8 driver / a man or a woman? ....?
9 you / see / a man in an old jacket on the corner?
   ....?
10 some men / repair / the road? ....?
11 anyone / wait / at the bus stop? ....?

Thank you, Mr Smith, that was very helpful.'

Now write Mr Smith's answers into a paragraph. Look at the picture to help you find the information.

Mr Smith told me that at 10.05 a.m. yesterday she (12) *was ouside the butcher's.* Joan Turner
(13) .... Mrs Jones (14) .... with her dog.
Mrs Walters (15) .... (16) .... robbers ....
the bank and they (17) .... guns. A big car (18) ....
and the driver (19) .... A man in an old jacket (20) ....
and some men (21) .... the road. Two children (22) ....
at the bus-stop.

Review (present and past, simple and continuous)

35   Look at this information about Marco and Jill.

Name:	Marco	Jill
Age:	15	29
Home town:	Rome	Dublin
Job:	Student	Computer programmer
Education/study:	12 subjects at school	Mathematics at university
Likes:	Playing football, cinema	Travelling, swimming, chocolate
Last holiday:	2 weeks in Greece last summer; hotel by the sea, lots of water sports	1 month in Indonesia last month; camping, lots of walking

Write questions about Marco. Use a verb in the present or past.

1   <u>How old is Marco?</u>   (old?)
2   <u>Where does he live?</u>   (live?)
3   .... (do?)
4   .... (study?)
5   .... (like?)
6   .... (last holiday?)
7   .... (stay?)
8   .... (do on holiday?)

Read the paragraph about Marco.

Marco is 15 and he comes from Rome. He is a student and is studying 12 subjects at school. He likes playing football and going to the cinema. Last summer he went to Greece for 2 weeks. He stayed in a hotel by the sea and he played lots of water sports.

Write a similar paragraph for Jill.

9   Jill is ....
....
....

☺   Now do the same for yourself.

I am ....
....
....

36 Complete the conversations. Put the verb in the correct form in the present or past.

1 JIM: (1) *Were* you *going* (go) shopping when I saw you yesterday morning?
　KATE: No, I (2) *was* on my way to the bank.
　JIM: I (3) *go* (go) to the bank every Friday, before the weekend.
　KATE: Me too usually. But this week I (4) *didn't have* (not / have) time, so I (5) *went* (go) yesterday.

2 JAN: (6) .... you .... (see) that science programme on TV last night?
　SAM: No, (7) .... never .... (watch) TV.
　JAN: It (8) .... wonderful. It (9) .... (show) a new way of repairing a heart.
　SAM: Oh.

3 JILL: Why (10) .... you .... (look) at me?
　TONY: Because you (11) .... (wear) a new dress and you look very good in it.
　JILL: Thank you. I (12) .... (buy) it yesterday.

4 VAL: What (13) .... Jim .... (do) this morning?
　IAN: He's at the doctor's at the moment.
　VAL: Oh dear. What (14) .... (happen)?
　IAN: He (15) .... (fall) and (16) .... (hurt) his leg yesterday when he (17) .... (run) for a bus.

5 VIC: (18) .... Sally .... (work) at half past seven last night?
　PAM: No, she (19) .... (help) me with the dinner. She often (20) .... (help) in the kitchen.
　VIC: When (21) .... she .... (go) out?
　PAM: She didn't. She (22) .... (stay) at home all evening.

37 Complete this conversation with a famous film actor. Put the verb into the correct form of the past or present.

INTERVIEWER: When (1) *did you start* (you / start) acting?
ACTOR: When I (2) .... (be) 12. I (3) .... (go) to a drama school, and one day I (4) .... (sit) in the classroom and Nigel Stewart, the famous film director, (5) .... (visit) the school. He (6) .... (see) me, and that (7) .... (be) the beginning.
INTERVIEWER: What (8) .... (be) your first film?
ACTOR: 'Holiday Home' with Terry Veale, who (9) .... (be) now my husband! We (10) .... (make) the film in Italy. He (11) .... (be) 17 and I (12) .... (be) 13!
INTERVIEWER: I know that Terry Veale (13) .... (have) an accident in that film. How (14) .... (it / happen)?
ACTOR: Well, one day near the end of the filming we (15) .... (both / ride) horses and Terry's horse suddenly (16) .... (stop) and he (17) .... (fall) off. He (18) .... (break) his arm. Today, Terry and I often (19) .... (talk) about our first meeting.
INTERVIEWER: (20) .... (you / ride) nowadays?
ACTOR: No, I (21) .... (stop) when I (22) .... (move) to Los Angeles.

INTERVIEWER: I know you are very busy but what (23) .... (you / do) in your
               free time?
ACTOR: Terry and I (24) .... (like) swimming. We (25) ....
               (swim) every day. And of course, I (26) .... (love) cooking. The
               dish I (27) .... (make) for lunch today is a new idea of mine.
INTERVIEWER: Can I ask you some more questions? And can I also talk to Terry?
ACTOR: Yes, of course. He (28) .... (swim) in our pool at the moment. We
               can go outside and enjoy the sun. Come on.

I have done (present perfect)

38   Complete the sentences. Use the present perfect in the correct form.

1   A: Is it raining at the moment? B: _No, it's just stopped_ (it / just / stop).
2   I can't find my keys. _Have you seen_ (you / see) them?
3   A: Where's your dictionary?
    B: I don't know .... (it / disappear).
4   A: Let's go and see 'Lions of Africa' at the Cannon cinema.
    B: .... (I / already / see) it.
    A: Oh well, ... (you / see) 'Green Beans'?
    B: No, let's go to that.
5   A: Please can I have my book back.
    B: Oh dear. .... (I / not / finish) it.
6   A: Are Steve and Martha at home? B: No, ... (they / go) out.
7   John looks thinner. .... (he / lose) weight?
8   A: Is Sally enjoying her new job?
    B: I don't know. .... (I / not / hear) from her.
9   A: Why doesn't this tape recorder work?
    B: I think .... (you / break) it.
10 Mary, you're very late. I was worried about you. Where ....
    (you / be)?
11 A: How many times .... (you / take) your driving test?
    B: Twice. My third one is next week.
12 This music is new to me. I'm sure .... (I / not / hear) it before.

39 Complete the sentences with **already** (I've already … / She's already …) or **yet** (He hasn't … yet / They haven't … yet).

1 MARK: Let's go to the new Spielman exhibition at the Modern Art Museum.
   JANE: I 've already seen it. It's not very good. (see)

2 DAVID: Don't forget to tell Mary the good news.
   LIZ: I .... and she was very happy. (tell)

3 SUE: What does John say in his letter?
   CHRIS: I don't know. I .... I've been too busy. (read)

4 TIM: Did Sue's operation go well?
   PAT: She .... The hospital were too busy. (have)

5 JOHN: I enjoyed reading that new novel by Sarah Dunmore. Is it her first book?
   JILL: No, she .... three, but I think this one is her best. (write)

6 PETE: Is that your father's new car?
   PAUL: Yes, it arrived last week but he .... (drive)

7 KATE: When are Tony and Chris going to sell their house?
   MICK: They .... They're moving to London next week. (sell)

40 You work for a travel agency. A customer, Jack, is interested in one of your walking holidays in the tropical rain forests of South America. You are asking him some questions beginning **Have you ever …?**

YOU:
1 Can you walk a long distance?
   Have you ever walked (walk) more than 40 kms?

2 Are you healthy?
   .... (have) a serious illness?
   .... (break) an arm or a leg?

3 Can you swim?
   .... (travel) in a canoe?

4 Do you like flying?
   .... (fly) in a helicopter?

5 Can you read a map?
   .... (lose) your way?

6 Do you sleep well?
   .... (sleep) outside?

7 Are you afraid of heights?
   .... (climb) a high mountain?

JACK:
Yes, no problem.
Yes, often.

Yes, very.
No, never.
My leg, twice.

Yes.
Yes, once.

Not very much.
Yes, a few times.

I think so.
No, never.

Yes, always.
Yes, many times.

No.
Yes, once.

Now write 3 sentences saying what Jack has done, and 3 sentences saying what Jack hasn't done

Jack has done a lot of things at different times in his life.
  He has (often) walked more than 40 kms, ...
but
  He has never ridden an elephant or a camel, ...

☺ And what about you?

  I've never walked more than 40 kms. ....

41 Put in **has/have been** or **has/have gone**.

1 HARRY: I saw you in Annabel's Restaurant last night
   DIANA: No, it wasn't me. I've... never ..been.... there.

2 SAM: Sally and Tim are on holiday, aren't they? Where .... they ....?
   SUE: To Florida, again.
   SAM: How many times .... they .... there?
   SUE: This is their third visit.

3 JOE: Can I have an apple, please?
   MARY: We haven't got any. I ....n't .... to the shops today.

4 ALAN: Where's Tony?
   MARK: He's got a headache so he .... to bed.

5 STEVE: (*on the phone*) Can I speak to Jill, please?
   LYNN: She's out, I'm afraid. She .... to the cinema this evening.
   STEVE: Again? She .... already .... to the cinema three times this week.

42 Complete the sentences using verbs in the present perfect.

> 'See that man over there? I'm sure I (1) 've seen....... him on TV. Oh yes, I remember, it's
> David Sen – the man I'm going to see at the Festival Hall tonight. He's a wonderful piano
> player. He and his family (2) .... a lot of different things in their lives. He
> (3) .... all over the world and he (4) .... many interesting
> people. He (5) .... a lot of money in piano-playing competitions so he's rich
> now. His daughter's only 20 and she (6) .... already .... a very
> successful cookery book and she's writing another one now. That's his son, Kenny, with
> him. He loves motorbikes. He (7) .... his bike all the way from Canada to
> Chile and he (8) .... just .... the story of his journey to a travel magazine.
> So *he'll* also be rich soon!
> David Sen's wife is a musician, too. She plays the flute. They (9) ....
> together many times in different countries. But they (10) .... never .... to
> our town before, so I'm going to their concert at the Festival Hall tonight.'
> 'You certainly know a lot about him!'

How long have you ...? (present perfect)

43   Complete the conversations. Make questions with **How long ...** + the present perfect simple.

1 PIPPA: Do you like London?
    MARTIN: Yes, very much.
    PIPPA: *How long have you lived* .... here? (live)

2 MIKE: This is a really good party, isn't it?
    JEAN: Yes, great.
    MIKE: .... here? (be)

3 PETE: Does Julie enjoy her work?
    LYNN: Not very much. She thinks the bank is a bit boring.
    PETE: .... there? (work)

4 TOM: Are you OK? You look a bit pale.
    LIZ: I've got a headache.
    TOM: .... it? (have)

5 ALEX: Did you know David and Sheila are going to get married in the autumn?
    JOHN: .... each other? (know)

6 SARAH: Today is Tom's last day at work. He doesn't want to stop but he's 65 next month so ...
    DAVID: .... with his company? (be)
    SARAH: All his working life.

44   **Since** or **for**? Put the following words and phrases into sentence 1 or sentence 2.

his birthday	~~Monday~~	more than 2 years	he left school
~~3 hours~~	a long time	this morning	2 o'clock yesterday
the beginning of April	Christmas	4 months	6 weeks 1992

1 Tony has worked here since ...   *Monday*

2 John has been married for ...   *3 hours*

45   Complete the sentences with a time phrase + **ago** (e.g. **2 hours ago**) or **for** + a time phrase (e.g. **for ten minutes**).

1 You can't be hungry. You had lunch *half an hour ago.*
2 Jane is fed up. She's been waiting *for a bus for an hour.*
3 I don't live in London now. I moved to New York ....
4 I now live in New York. I've been here ....
5 Tom's grandparents died ....
6 Tims got 'flu. He's been in bed ....
7 Jane and William got married .... and their first child was born
....
8 I like Mary's hair. She's had it in that style ....

48 Write complete sentences. Use the present perfect and the past simple.

1 You / be / tired / all day. What time / you / go to bed / last night?
   You've been tired all day. What time did you go to bed last night?

2 Francis / leave / home / 6 o'clock this morning. He / drive / since then.
   Francis left home at 6 o'clock this morning. He has been driving since then.

3 Brasilia / the capital of Brazil / since 1960. Before 1960, Rio de Janeiro / the capital.

4 Carol / move / to Oxford / in 1975. She / live / in Oxford / since 1975.

5 I / not / see / the new manager / yet. When / she / start working for the company?

6 You / speak / good French / on the telephone / yesterday. How long / you / learn / it?

7 Paula and Laurence / be / married / since last year. They / meet / at university.

8 Peter / never / try / Japanese food. He / go Japan / last year but he / eat / hamburgers.

9 I / break my arm / six months ago. I / use / a computer for my work / since then.

10 My brother / be / a professional footballer / since 1994. But when he / be / younger he /
   not / like / sport very much.

49 Put the verb in the present perfect or the past simple.

Here is the six o'clock news from ITC, on Monday the 25th April.
Our reporter in Nepal (1) __telephoned__ (telephone) us ten minutes ago and (2) __said__ (say) that
Jane Tomkins and her partner, Ann Beckett, are on top of the world today. They
(3) .... (reach) the top of Mount Everest half hour ago. Our reporter spoke
to another climber on the expedition.

REPORTER: Are Jane and Ann still on the top of Mount Everest?
CLIMBER: No, they (4) .... (start) their return journey.
REPORTER: How long (5) .... they .... (spend) up there?
CLIMBER: About 10 minutes. They (6) .... (take) some photographs of
            each other.
REPORTER: Are they in good health?
CLIMBER: Well, they're both tired, but they're fine. But there is one problem: the weather
            (7) .... (change). There is more cloud and the wind is quite
            strong.

Last night, Manchester United (8) .... (win) the football league
championship. The team (9) .... (win) the championship three times now –
the first time (10) .... (be) in 1986. In their final game yesterday, Bryan
Riggs (11) .... (score) the winning goal. Riggs (12) .... (be)
with the team since he (13) .... (leave) school.

The President of Volponia, Madame Fernoff, (14) .... (arrive) in Britain last
night. Madame Fernoff (15) .... (be) President since 1985. She said she was
very happy to be in Britain.

At yesterday's meeting of European finance ministers, Jack Delaney, the Irish Finance Minister,
(16) .... (say), 'I am going to leave my job soon. I
(17) .... (work) very hard and I want to spend more time with my family.'
Mr Delaney (18) .... (be) Irish Finance Minister for 5 years.

And the weather. We (19) .... (have) a lot of rain over the country since the
beginning of the week and unfortunately this will continue until the weekend. For your
information, last week (20) .... (be) the wettest April week for 100 years.

50   Complete the dialogues. Use the present perfect or the past simple of the verbs in brackets ( ).

1 CLARE: *Have* .... you .. *seen* .... (see) John?
   COLIN: No, why?
   CLARE: He's *broken* .... (break) his leg.
   COLIN: Really? When *did* .. he .. *do* .. (do) that?
   CLARE: Yesterday.

2 ADAM: Oh no! I .... (lose) my car keys.
   TONY: When .... you last .... (see) them?
   ADAM: This morning when I .... (leave) the house.

3 MARY: Alan's going to sell his car.
   SIMON: Really? He only .... (buy) it last month.
   MARY: I know. He loves changing cars.
   SIMON: How many cars .... he .... (have) in his life?
   MARY: At least 20!

4 BEN: Can I look at the newspaper, please?
   VAL: In a minute. I .... (not / finish) with it yet.
   BEN: You're very slow. You .... (start) it this morning after
        breakfast!

5 JULIA: There was a good programme on TV last night about elephants.
        .... you .... (see) it?
   SARAH: Yes, it was wonderful. .... you ever .... (see) a *live* elephant?
   JULIA: Yes, and I .... (touch) one, too.
   SARAH: When .... (be) that?
   JULIA: Two years ago when I .... (be) on holiday in Kenya.

6 PATRICK: Connie looks really fed up. What's the matter?
   JOSIE: She .... (fail) her driving test yesterday.
   PATRICK: Not again! How many times .... she .... (fail)?
   JOSIE: I think it's four.

Review (present, present perfect and past)

51 Follow the instructions for each exercise.

A Choose the right answer.

At 11 o'clock yesterday morning, John (1) <u>was</u> / ~~has been~~
sitting in the waiting room at the doctor's. Next to him
(2) <u>is/was</u> a woman with a very large thumb.
(3) 'How <u>did you do</u> / <u>were you doing</u> that?' John asked.
(4) 'I <u>hung</u> / <u>was hanging</u> a picture on the wall and I
(5) <u>hit</u> / <u>was hitting</u> my thumb by mistake.'
(6) 'Oh dear. How long (6) <u>have you been</u> / <u>are you</u> waiting
for the doctor?'
'About an hour, and my thumb (7) <u>is hurting</u> / <u>has hurt</u> a lot.'

B Put the verb in brackets ( ) in the correct tense.

Mary usually (8) ..**takes**.... (take) a bus to the office but today she (9) ....
(drive) because she is late. Last night her manager (10) .... (telephone) her
and (11) .... (ask) her to be at the office at 8.30 a.m. for an important
meeting. 'I (12) .... late (never / be) for a meeting in my life. Why
(13) .... (my mother / forget) to wake me this morning?'

C Complete the questions.

MARK: (14) ..**What's**.... your job?
PETE: I'm an engineer with National Telephones.
MARK: How long (15) .... for that company?
PETE: About 9 months.
MARK: (16) .... it?
PETE: No, not really. I preferred my old job.
MARK: What (17) .... that?
PETE: I was a gardener.

CHRIS: (18) .... ever .... an accident?
ANNE: Yes, once a few years ago.
CHRIS: How (19) ....?
ANNE: I was driving too fast.
CHRIS: (20) .... a bad accident?
ANNE: Not very bad. I broke my arm but the other driver was OK.
CHRIS: Why (21) .... fast now?
ANNE: I'm not! This is my normal speed in a town.

TOM: Why (22) .... at me?
RUTH: Because you've got a bit of tomato on your face.
TOM: Where (23) .... it?
RUTH: On the right of your nose.
TOM: (24) .... or is it still there?
RUTH: It's still there.

52 Read the letter from Chris to her friend, Jo. Chris is from San Francisco and has just had a holiday with Jo in London. Complete the sentences. Put the verb in brackets in the correct form.

> Dear Jo
> Well, I (1) _arrived_ (arrive) back safely two weeks ago. The flight
> (2) .... (be) *fine, but a bit long. I* (3) .... (watch)
> *two films and* (4) .... (eat) *two breakfasts!*
>   *Thank you for everything. I* (5) .... (have) *a really good time with*
> *you in London. I hope you* (6) .... (enjoy) *it too.*
>   *Everything here is very different from London. I* (7) .... (write) *this*
> *letter outside in the garden. I* (8) .... (sit) *under a big umbrella because*
> *the sun is very hot today. I know we* (9) .... (have) *some sunny days in*
> *London but I remember there* (10) .... (be) *also some rain!*
>   *It was difficult for me to start work after my wonderful holiday, but it's OK now. I*
> (11) .... (be) *in a new department since I* (12) ....
> (come) *home and it's interesting. I* (13) .... (have) *a new manager*
> *now, and that's good because the old one* (14) .... (be) *horrible.*
>   (15) .... (you / like) *rock music? My brother* (16) ....
> (be) *a drummer in a new group. He* (17) .... (practise) *in his bedroom at*
> *the moment and it's quite loud! I* (18) .... (just / send) *you some of his*
> *cassettes. I hope you like them.*
>   *By the way,* (19) .... (you / find) *a black leather photo album? I*
> *think I* (20) .... (leave) *it in the bedroom. Could you send it to me*
> *sometime? No hurry.*
>   *Jill* (21) .... (sit) *in the garden with me and she sends her love to*
> *you. Please write soon, and thank you again for a wonderful time.*
>   *Love Chris*

Now write Jo's reply in complete sentences.

Dear Chris

22 Thank you for your letter. Yes, I / enjoy / the time you / spend / with me very much. We / have / some good fun!
  Thank you for your letter. Yes, I enjoyed the time ....

23 You / leave / a wonderful box of chocolates for my parents. Thank you. We / just / finish / them – they / be delicious.

24 And thank you also for the cassettes. They / arrive / yesterday. I / not / play / all of them yet. At the moment I / listen / to one, 'Paradise Rock'. It / be / very good.

25　My mother / find / your photo album the day you / leave. I / send / it back two weeks ago. you / receive / it yet?

....

....

26　Do you remember Steve? We / meet / him at Sue's party. Well, he / come / to my house last week. He / ask / for your address so I / give / it to him. I hope that's OK. He / be / in California now on business.

....

....

27　I / look / out of the window at the moment. The sun / shine and it / be / a beautiful, warm day. In fact, it / be / sunny / every day since you / go back / to San Francisco. Sorry!

....

....

28　The cassette / just / finish. Tell your brother I love his music. he / want / a publicity agent in London?

....

....

That's all for now. Write soon.
Love
Jo

☺ Last week you stayed with a friend for a few days, but now you are home again. Write a 'thank you' letter to the friend. Use the following points and the letter from Chris to Jo to help you.

– thank the friend
– write about the journey home
– write about the things you enjoyed when you were with your friend
– you are sending a present – tell / him her about it
– write what you're doing now
– ask her / him to write to you

is done / was done and is being done / has been done (passive)

Units 21–22

53　Write the quiz questions. Use the past simple passive.

QUIZ MASTER: Welcome to our General Knowledge Quiz. We've got some interesting questions for you tonight, Marianne, so are you ready?
MARIANNE: Ready.
QUIZ MASTER: OK, number 1: When (1) *was* the toothbrush *invented* (invent)? Was it the 15th or the 17th century?
MARIANNE: The 15th century, I think – in China.
QUIZ MASTER: That's right. Number 2: Where (2) .... compact discs .... (develop)?
MARIANNE: In Japan.
QUIZ MASTER: Japan and The Netherlands together, actually. And number 3: (3) .... dynamite .... (invent) in Canada, Sweden or Greece?

MARIANNE:	In Sweden by Alfred Nobel.
QUIZ MASTER:	OK, Number 4: in which century (4) .... glasses first .... (make)?
MARIANNE:	I'm not sure. The 15th century?
QUIZ MASTER:	No, I'm sorry. It was in the 13th century by two Italians. And for your fifth question: When (5) .... contact lenses first .... (produce)?
MARIANNE:	1956.
QUIZ MASTER:	Correct. And your last question: Where (6) .... the first petrol car ....? (build)
MARIANNE:	In Germany by Mr Daimler and Mr Benz.
QUIZ MASTER:	That's right. Congratulations, Marianne. You did very well.

54 Look at the picture of Hartson's jam factory. A visitor is being shown around the factory by Mr Jones, the manager. Complete his sentences. Use the passive (present simple or continuous).

The machines (1) **are switched on** (switch on) at 7.30 a.m. every day and (2) **(are) turned off** (turn off) at 5.30 p.m. The factory (3) .... (lock) at 6.30 p.m. by our security guards and all the staff (4) .... (check) before they go home. We don't want our jam to disappear! Now as you can see, strawberry jam (5) .... (make) here today. And over there the jars of jam (6) .... (put) into boxes by our team. Hartson's jam (7) .... (not / export) because this country buys everything we produce. It's very important to keep our factory clean and hygienic so everything (8) .... (wash) very carefully every night. Of course nobody (9) .... (allow) to smoke anywhere in the factory. Now I think lunch (10) .... (serve) in the canteen at the moment, so shall we go?

55   First, look at picture 1. Then, look at picture 2. Write what has been done and what hasn't. Four things are different and three things are the same. Use the verbs in the box.

| wash | close | ~~finish~~ | repair | turn off | turn off | ~~throw away~~ |

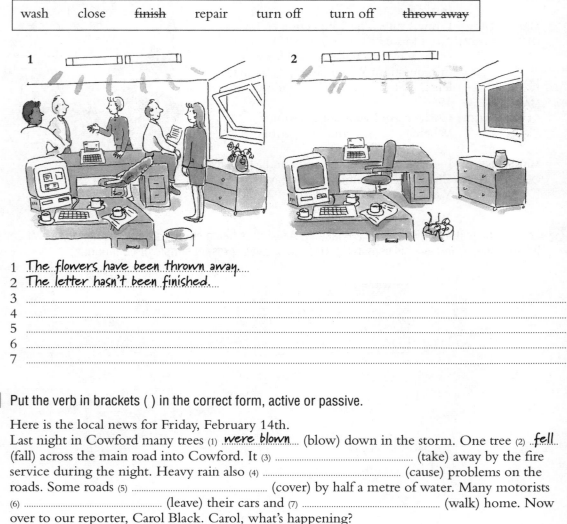

1   *The flowers have been thrown away.*
2   *The letter hasn't been finished.*
3   ....
4   ....
5   ....
6   ....
7   ....

56   Put the verb in brackets ( ) in the correct form, active or passive.

Here is the local news for Friday, February 14th.
Last night in Cowford many trees (1) *were blown* (blow) down in the storm. One tree (2) *fell* (fall) across the main road into Cowford. It (3) .... (take) away by the fire service during the night. Heavy rain also (4) .... (cause) problems on the roads. Some roads (5) .... (cover) by half a metre of water. Many motorists (6) .... (leave) their cars and (7) .... (walk) home. Now over to our reporter, Carol Black. Carol, what's happening?

Well, the situation this morning is better, and nearly back to normal. The last few cars (8) .... (remove) by the emergency services at the moment. And I can see the telephone engineers at work. The broken lines (9) .... (repair). The traffic (10) .... now .... (move) in and out of the town along the main roads.

Thank you Carol. And now one piece of good news.
Yesterday evening, a black BMW (11) .... (steal) from outside the home of Mr John Simpson. Mr Simpson (12) .... (telephone) the police. Later that evening, the car (13) .... (see) in the High Street by Mr Simpson's wife, Laura. It was outside the Red Lion Hotel. The keys were in the car, so she (14) .... (drive) it home! The police (15) .... (look) for a careless thief!

And finally, some football news.
We (16) .... just .... (hear) that Cowford Town are champions for the fourth time! A few minutes ago the referee (17) .... (blow) the whistle at the end of the game against Grimeton. Our reporter at the match, Kevin Anderson, (18) .... (wait) to talk to us at the stadium.

STUDIO: Kevin, (19) .... (be) it a good game?
KEVIN: Yes, excellent, very fast but unfortunately a bit rough. Cowford's star player, Tony Ancock (20) .... (send) off because he (21) .... (kick) one of the Grimeton players. And the Grimeton goalkeeper (22) .... (hurt) when he (23) .... (crash) into one of the goalposts. He (24) .... (take) off the field with leg injuries, so both teams (25) .... (play) with ten men for the last few minutes.
STUDIO: Is he all right?
KEVIN: Well, we don't know. He (26) .... (take) to hospital at this moment. The manager (27) .... (think) it's serious.
STUDIO: Oh dear. That's a bad end to the match for Grimeton. What (28) .... (happen) now in the stadium?
KEVIN: The Cowford players (29) .... (walk) up the steps to receive the Champions Cup. And now back to the studio.

be/have/do and regular/irregular verbs   Units 23–24

57 Complete the sentences using the verbs in the box.

has	weren't	is	haven't	didn't	doesn't	are	was	~~am~~	were

1 I am.. starting university in the autumn.
2 Frank isn't at work at the moment. He .... gone to Switzerland for a conference.
3 The Channel Tunnel .... built between 1985 and 1994.
4 Phillip .... eat meat. He's a vegetarian.
5 We .... been to Toronto before. This is our first time in Canada.
6 Look! Our cat .... playing with the dog from next door!
7 Your jeans .... washed last week and now they're dirty again!
8 I turned the stereo off because you .... listening to it.
9 A lot of leather shoes .... imported from Italy.
10 I .... go out last night.

58 Write the questions. Use **were you**, **did they**, **has he**, etc.

1 JEAN: When _were you_ born?
   FRED: May 29th, 1964.

2 STEVE: .... need an umbrella?
   JULIA: No, it isn't raining at the moment.

3 DENISE: .... coming to Jane's party tomorrow?
   HAZEL: Yes, I think so.

4 MIKE: I must go to the shops. What time .... close?
   CAROL: At 5.30.

5 ADAM: .... read John Presley's new book yet?
   MARY: No, I haven't. Is it good?

6 VAL: When .... get married?
   LIZ: A long time ago. When I was 21.

7 ED: I'm really sorry your car has gone. When .... stolen?
   FRANK: Yesterday. It was parked in the street outside my house.

8 LYNN: .... been in hospital before?
   LISA: No, this is her first time, and she's a bit worried.

9 MARK: .... waiting for a bus when I saw you last night?
   SARAH: No, a taxi.

59 Put the verb in brackets ( ) into the right form. Use the past simple (e.g. **sold**, **broke**, etc.) and past participle (e.g. **rung**, **gone**, etc.).

1 Sue _sold_ her motorbike when she _broke_ her leg last year. (sell / break)

2 I've _rung_ the doorbell three times and there's no answer. I think they've _gone_ out. (ring / go)

3 I .... the letter to Ruth but she .... to post it. (give / forget)

4 Ian hasn't .... his keys yet. He can't remember where he .... them. (find / leave)

5 Do you remember the photograph of Don that you .... me? Was it .... by a professional photographer? (show / take)

6 A lion .... from the national zoo yesterday but it was .... a few hours later. (escape / catch)

7 James has often .... about flying in a helicopter but he hasn't .... it yet. (think / do)

8 When she was younger, Paula always .... a ring which was .... to her by her grandmother. (wear / give)

9 Alan .... to swim when he was a baby. But he .... into a river when he was four years old and he has never .... again. (learn / fall / swim)

10 Jill .... ill last night so she .... to bed and .... for ten hours. (feel / go / sleep)

11 When I was younger, a teacher at my school .... me. It .... a lot and I have never .... it. (hit / hurt / forget)

I used to …

60 Complete the sentences. Use **used to** and a suitable verb.

George Medley is listening to a guide telling a group of visitors about the town of Stampford.
He is thinking about Stampford in the past.

GEORGE
MEDLEY

GUIDE:

Stampford is a very busy town nowadays.
There are lots of things to do.
For example, we have a big new cinema
complex.
And this is the chemical factory. It's very
important for the town. A lot of people
work here.
Unfortunately, the river is not very clean
now.
Broad Street is the main shopping street in
town.
We now have a wonderful cheap bus
service.
And of course, we've got lots of fast food
restaurants.
And look, there's Paul Carr, our famous
artist.
As you can see, Stampford is a good place
to live.

GEORGE MEDLEY:

1 _It used to be_ very quiet.

2 It .... a school.

3 I .... football in the
   park there.

4 I .... in that river.

5 Our family .... at
   number 23.
6 Everyone .... to the
   shops.
7 We .... at home.

8 He .... a waiter.

9 It .... better.

☺ Can you think of four things that you **used to do** when you were younger that you don't do now?
You can use the following verbs to help you: live / play / speak / go / like / listen.

10 ....
11 ....
12 ....
13 ....

61 Read the text about the Inuit people of North America and complete it with the verbs below.
Use **used to** or the present simple (e.g. **he lives**, **they have**, etc.).

| have | drive | wear | wear | live | take off | be |
| cook | ~~call~~ | hunt | go | take | hate | spend |

IGLOO

SEAL

SNOWSHOES

FUR

The lives of the Inuit people of North America have changed a lot in 30 years.

First, their name: people (1) _used to call_ them Eskimos, but now they are called Inuits, which means 'the people'.

They (2) .... in igloos in the winter but today, many of them live in houses in small towns. They (3) .... seals – they ate the meat and made clothes from the fur. Many of the people still (4) .... seal-skin clothes today because they are very warm. Remember, the weather is extremely cold for many months of the year. 85-year-old Inuit, Mariano Tagalik, told us a little about her early life.

'Our winter igloos were very warm. We (5) .... inside so sometimes it got too hot. When I was a child I (6) .... most of my clothes when I was in our igloo. In the short summers we lived in seal-skin tents, but I (7) .... as much time as possible playing outside.'

To move over the snow, they (8) .... special snowshoes on their feet, but today many Inuits (9) .... snowmobiles. These machines can travel long distances in a short time. In the past it (10) .... them days or weeks to travel the same distance.

Inuit children never (11) .... to school – they learnt everything from their parents but now, like all North Americans, they (12) .... about 10 years of school education.

Life is not as hard as it (13) ...., but many of the older Inuits (14) .... town life and want to go back to the old days.

What are you doing tomorrow?

62 Complete the conversation. Use the present continuous (e.g. **he's coming**) or the present simple (e.g. **he comes**).

Josie Turner is the export manager of a large international company. Harry Brentwood is a customer from Canada. They are trying to arrange an appointment for next week.

JOSIE: Hello, Josie Turner speaking.

HARRY: Oh Josie, this is Harry Brentwood. How are you? I (1) __'m coming__ (come) to London on Sunday and I'd like to meet you next week. Can we arrange a time?

JOSIE: I'd love to. When are you free?

HARRY: Well how about lunch on Monday?

JOSIE: I can't, I'm afraid. I (2) .... (have) lunch with our new Chairman. Tuesday at 10.30?

HARRY: No, no good. Dennis, my London agent, (3) .... (come) to the office. Wednesday afternoon is a possibility.

JOSIE: Not for me. My secretary, Jenny, (4) .... (get married) and all of us (5) .... (go) to the wedding. And on Thursday morning I (6) .... (drive) up to Manchester for a meeting with Bill Syms.

HARRY: What time (7) .... the meeting .... (start)?

JOSIE: 11.30 a.m. I've got an idea! Why don't you come with me? We can talk on the way.

HARRY: That sounds good. Oh, but wait a minute, I can't. I (8) .... (talk) to a group of business people about Canadian business opportunities at lunchtime.

JOSIE: So Friday, then.

HARRY: Yes. That's the only possibility because my return flight to Montreal (9) .... (leave) at 9.00 a.m. on Saturday. So, 11.30 a.m. on Friday morning at your office?

JOSIE: Yes, that's perfect. I'm really looking forward to seeing you then.

☺ Some friends of yours invite you to different things next week but you can't go to any of them because you're busy. Write what you are doing at those times. Use the present continuous (e.g. **I'm having**).

10 A: There's a party at my house on Tuesday night. Would you like to come?
   B: I can't, I'm afraid. __I'm having dinner with Mary.__

11 A: Meet me on Wednesday evening in the city centre.
   B: I can't ....

12 A: See you on Friday at 12.30 p.m. outside the museum. OK?
   B: I can't ....

13 A: Jim wants you to come to the cinema with us on Saturday afternoon.
   B: I can't ....

14 A: Let's go for a walk on Sunday.
   B: I can't ....

63   Use the words below to write complete sentences or questions. Use the present continuous or the present simple.

1 A: Let's meet outside the cinema.
    B: What time / the film / start?
       What time does the film start?
    A: At 7.15 p.m.

2 A: What time / you / go / on Friday?
       What time are you going on Friday?
    B: After lunch.

3 A: Hurry up! We're late. The next bus / leave / in five minutes.
    ....
    B: OK, I'm ready.

4 A: Where / you / go / at the weekend?
    ....?
    B: I don't know yet.

5 A: Let's get a taxi home after the concert.
    B: Why? It / not / finish late.
    ....

6 A: Jane / work at Brown's Restaurant tonight so she can't come to the party.
    ....
    B: Oh, that's a pity.

7 A: Why's Frank in bed so early tonight?
    B: He / leave / for France at 5 a.m. tomorrow.
    ....

8 A: Where / the next train / go to?
    ....?
    B: Bristol, I think.

I'm going to …

64   Write questions with … **going to** … .

1 BEN: what / Dad / do?   _What's Dad going to do?_
   MUM: Paint the kitchen walls.
   BEN: what colour / he / do them?   _What colour's he going to do them?_
   MUM: White.

2 JILL: what / you / buy / for Paul's birthday? ....?
  MEG: I don't know yet.
  JILL: he / have / a party? ....?
  MEG: Yes, on Saturday.
3 TOM: you / buy / a new computer? ....?
  SUE: Yes.
  TOM: what kind / you / get? ....?
  SUE: An Apple Mac, I think.
4 MARY: what / Sarah / do / after university? ....?
  JACK: First, she's going to travel.
  MARY: how long / she / be away? ....?
  JACK: About six months.
5 PAUL: Joe and Kate / get married? ....?
  SALLY: Yes, in the autumn.
  PAUL: where / they / live? ....?
  SALLY: With her parents.

65 Write sentences using … **going to** (**be**) …

1 It's only 7 o'clock in the morning but the sun is shining and it's warm.
   It's going to be a beautiful day.
2 John is driving on the wrong side of the road! .... an accident!
3 Carol is eating her third box of chocolates! .... sick!
4 What a fantastic race! Roger is nearly there! Only 50 metres to the finish.
   .... win!
5 Look at those boys on that big bicycle! They're not safe. .... fall
   off!
6 This film is making me feel very sad. .... cry.

will/shall

66 Read what George says about his life at the moment and his future.

> *Friday 25th*
>
> At the moment I have to work very hard. I study at home every night and tonight is the same. I'll be at home as usual. I'll be in my bedroom with my books.
>
> But tomorrow is Saturday - no college and no work! So tomorrow morning I'll probably be in the city centre. I want to buy some clothes.
>
> College finishes next month so at the end of the month I'll be on holiday in Paris with my friends.
>
> A few years from now I'll probably be married.
>
> In 2010 I'll be 40 years old. My children will probably be at school.
>
> I don't know where I'll be in 2020.

Are these statements true? Correct the sentences that are wrong. Use **will** and **won't**.

1 George'll be at the cinema this evening. _No, he won't. He'll be at home._
2 He'll be in his bedroom. _True_
3 Tomorrow morning he'll be at college. _____
4 Next month he'll be in Paris. _____
5 He'll be on his own. _____
6 A few years from now, he'll probably be married. _____
7 He'll be 28 in 2001. _____
8 His children will probably be at university. _____
9 He'll be in Paris in 2020. _____

☺ And you? Where will you be? Write sentences about yourself. Use **I'll be … / I'll probably be … / I don't know where I'll be**.

This evening _____
Tomorrow morning _____
Next month _____
A few years from now _____
In 2010 _____

67 Complete the sentences. Use **will** (**'ll**) or **won't** + a verb from the box.

see	tell	~~win~~	stay	get

1 JANE: I'm going to the big baseball match tonight. My team, Dallas Cowboys, are playing.
 BEN: Do you think they *'ll win?*
 JANE: Of course. They're the best!

2 KATH: The new man in the sales department doesn't look very happy.
 LUCY: No, I don't think he .... very long.

3 PAT: Don't say anything to John about the surprise party on Saturday.
 SUE: Don't worry. I .... him.

4 FRED: You look sad. What's the matter?
 ZOE: My grandparents are on their way to Australia. They're going to live there, so I
 probably .... again.
 FRED: Why not? You can go there for a holiday.

5 SAM: Tony and Maria have known each other for a long time.
 TINA: Yes. I think they .... married soon.
 SAM: I don't think so. They haven't got any money.

68 Your grandmother has a few problems.
Offer to help her.
Write sentences with **Shall I ...?**

My eyes are not good. I can't read Jane's letter.	1	*Shall I read* it to you?
I'm thirsty.	2	.... you a cup of tea?
It's a bit cold in here.	3	.... the window?
I can't open this packet of biscuits.	4	.... it for you?
I can't hear what that man on TV is saying.	5	.... it up?
The dog needs some exercise.	6	.... him for a walk?
I think the kitchen floor is dirty.	7	.... it for you?

69 Joe and Phil went camping in Portugal last year. Now they are planning their next holiday. Write
questions with **Shall we ...?** Look at the answers first.

JOE: It's time to start planning this summer's holiday. Where (1) *shall we go?*

PHIL: Let's go to Portugal again. I enjoyed it last year.

JOE: (2) .... in the same hotel?

PHIL: No, let's try something different. How about camping?

JOE: Great! I bought a new tent last year. (3) .... that?

PHIL: Yes, let's. (4) .... or fly?

JOE: Oh, drive I think because we'll have a lot of luggage.

PHIL: When (5) ....?

JOE: The middle of July is best for me. How about you?

PHIL: July is fine for me, too. (6) .... Tony to come with us?

JOE: No. The tent is only big enough for two people!

Review (future)

70   Put the verb in the present continuous (e.g. **they're going**) or the present simple (e.g. **I see**).

1   I usually ..*see*.. (see) my parents at the weekend but this weekend I can't because they ..*are going*.. (go) to London.

2   Julian .... (have) a holiday later this year. Normally he .... (go) on holiday in July, but this year he can't.

3   Sue .... (not / often / stay) at home in the evenings but tonight she .... (stay) in because there's an important football match on TV.

4   .... (you / take) your exam next month? .... (you / want) to borrow my notes?

5   I .... (cook) the meals this weekend. Normally, Jane .... (do) it but she's away all weekend.

71   What do you say in the following situations? Use **will** or the present continuous.

1   Jane tells you she cannot play tennis tonight because her partner is ill. You offer to play with her. What do you say? ..*I'll play with you.*..

2   Your young brother breaks his favourite toy train. He's very sad. You offer to buy him another one. What do you say? ....

3   You and your sister have arranged to go shopping tomorrow. A friend invites you to lunch. What do you say? I can't come ....

4   You're flying to Athens this afternoon. Your mother wants to know that you have arrived safely. You offer to telephone her this evening. What do you say?

....

5   Your brother, Tony, and his wife, Rachel, come to dinner once a week at your house. Tonight is the night. What do you say to your mother?
Don't forget that ....

6   Frank wants to go to the cinema to see 'Black Nights'. It's a horror film and you know he doesn't like horror films. What do you say to him?
I don't think ....

7   Julia wants to know about your weekend plans. What does she ask you?
.... at the weekend?

8   Your plan is to stay at home all weekend. What do you say to Julia?
.... all weekend.

72   Are the underlined words right or wrong? Correct the sentences that are wrong.

1   The new road <u>shall</u> be open in the summer.   *The road will be open in the summer.*

2   The exam <u>starts</u> at 8.30 tomorrow.   ..*right*..

3   I've got my ticket. I <u>will go</u> to Spain. ....

4   You look tired. Sit down. I'm <u>making</u> you a cup of coffee. ....

5   What time <u>is</u> the sun <u>rising</u> tomorrow? ....

6   Where <u>do you go</u> for lunch today? ....

7   <u>Shall we learn</u> Spanish next year? ....

8   Do you think it <u>is raining</u> later? ....

9   I can't come because <u>I'll be</u> on holiday. ....

10 (on the phone) It's Ann you want to speak to. Just one minute, please. <u>I'm going to call</u> her.

11 Don't worry about me, Mum. <u>I'll write</u> to you every day from the States.

73 Write complete sentences.

1 **present continuous or will?**
JANE: What did Jack say on the phone?
ANNE: He / have / a party on Saturday.
   He's having a party on Saturday.
JANE: you / go? *Are you going?*
ANNE: Yes. I like Jack's parties.
JANE: Did he invite me, too?
ANNE: Yes, but you can't come, can you?
JANE: No, I / be / away at the weekend.
   No, I'll be away at the weekend.

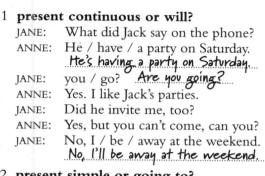

2 **present simple or going to?**
TOM: Great! That's the end of school for a few weeks.
LUCY: When / the next term / begin? ....?
TOM: On September 3rd.
LUCY: What / you do / during the holidays? ....?
TOM: I don't know yet. What about you?
LUCY: I / not / finish / until next week. Then, I / look / for a job for the summer.
....

3 **will or going to?**
VAL: Do you want to play tennis on Friday?
BEN: I can't. I / visit my grandmother. ....
VAL: Does she live near?
BEN: Not really. About 100 kms away. But my car isn't working at the moment. I / take it to the garage. ....
VAL: I / lend you mine. I don't need it on Friday. ....
BEN: Oh, thank you, I / buy the petrol. ....

4 **present continuous or will?**
JACK: everybody / come / to the meeting on Friday afternoon?
..................?
PAM: Most people.
JACK: you think / it / be a long meeting? ....?
PAM: I'm not sure. It / probably / be about 3 hours. Why?
JACK: I / go to the dentist at 5.30. I made the appointment two weeks ago.
....

might

74 A friend is asking you about some plans. You're not sure. Use **might** (**not**).

1 A: Where are you going this weekend?
   B: I don't know yet. _I might go to Tim's party_ (Tim's party)
      but _I might not go anywhere_ (not / anywhere).

2 A: It's a national holiday tomorrow so there's no public transport. How are Jane and Sue
      going to get there?
   B: I don't know. It'll be difficult. They _____ (taxi)
      but _____ (not / come).

3 A: Who are you going to invite to dinner?
   B: I haven't decided yet. _____ (Sarah)
      but _____ (not / Tony).

4 A: What new clothes does Clare want to buy on Saturday?
   B: She's not sure yet. _____ (some jeans)
      but _____ (not / anything).

☺ What about you? What are you going to do this weekend? Use **might** (**not**) in your answers.

5 _I might go to the cinema._   7 _____
6 _____   8 _____

75 Read this information about Peter's holiday. Write sentences with (**not**) **going to** and **might** (**not**).

Peter's going on holiday tomorrow. He's packed his suitcases and he's ready to leave early in the
morning. He's going to China. It's going to be a busy holiday because there are a lot of things he
wants to do and see, and some things he hasn't decided about yet.

sure	**perhaps**
1 Visit the Forbidden City, Beijing	2 Not have time to visit the museums
3 Walk along The Great Wall	4 Try the rice wine
5 Not eat western food	6 Go on a boat trip
7 Learn a few phrases of Chinese	8 Not come home!

1 _Peter is going to visit the Forbidden City in Beijing._
2 _He might not have time to visit the museums._
3 _____
4 _____
5 _____
6 _____
7 _____
8 _____

can and could

76 Paula has got a problem. Use **can** or **can't** + the verb in brackets ( ).

Oh dear! Where's my key? I (1) *can't find* (find) it. Oh look! It's on the kitchen table. I
(2) .... (see) it. Now what am I going to do? I (3) .... (get) in. I
(4) .... (climb) the tree to the window on the first floor. It's too high. I
(5) .... (telephone) for help because I haven't got my money with me. Hey, what's
that noise in the sitting room? I (6) .... (hear) something. Oh good, it's Peter. He's
at home. I'm safe!

The next day, Peter tells his friend, Kate, about Paula's problem.
7 Paula *couldn't find* her key yesterday.
8 She .... it on the kitchen table.
9 She .... in.
10 She .... the tree.
11 She .... for help.
12 She .... someone in the sitting room – it was me!

77 Complete these sentences. Use **can't** or **couldn't** + a verb from the box.

type	see	speak	~~find~~	come
catch	~~sleep~~	answer	understand	

1 I'd like to read Jim's letter. The only problem is I *can't find* my glasses.
2 Kevin was really tired last night but he *couldn't sleep.*
3 Jane would like to work in an office, but unfortunately she ....
4 People said he was a very interesting speaker, but I .... him.
5 Sue didn't pass her Maths exam because she .... the questions.
6 I've got two tickets for the ballet on Saturday, but unfortunately Frank
....
7 Maria's dog ran out of the house and she .... it.
8 A: I'd like to live in Paris. B: Me too, but I .... French very well.
9 (*at the cinema*) Those people in front of me are very tall. I .... the screen.

78 You are staying in a hotel. What do you say in these situations? Use **Can / Could you ...?** or **Can / Could I ...?**

1 You want the receptionist to turn the air-conditioning off in your room because you're cold.
Could you (or Can you) turn the air-conditioning off, please?

2 There is only one towel in your room. You want another one.
Can I (or Could I) have another towel, please?

3 You want the receptionist to give you a wake-up call at 6.30 in the morning.
....?

4 You want breakfast in your room tomorrow morning.
....?

5 You want to leave your passport and travellers cheques in the hotel safe.
....?

6 There is no hair dryer in your room. You want to borrow one.
....?

7 You want the receptionist to get a taxi for you.
....?

must/mustn't/needn't Unit 32

79 Complete each sentence. Use **must / mustn't / had to** + a verb.

1 Jill and Terry will be home from school soon. I *must cook* their lunch.
2 Derek .... late at the office last night. There was an important job to do.
3 If you are absent for more than three days, you .... a letter from your doctor.
4 The dentist has told Alan he .... any more sweet things. His teeth are in bad condition.
5 When Barbara was five years old, she .... to school, but she didn't want to.
6 Let's catch an earlier train tomorrow. We .... late for the meeting.
7 My hair feels really dirty. I .... it tonight.
8 I forgot my front door key yesterday so I .... into the house through a window.

80 Complete the sentences. Use **mustn't** or **needn't** + a verb from the box. Use each verb twice.

~~help~~	ask	read	leave	work

1 Carol *mustn't help* you with your homework. It's important that you do it yourself.
2 You *needn't help* with the shopping. John has already done it.
3 We .... Bill about his holiday. He doesn't want to talk about it.
4 I just want a general idea of the story so I .... all the book.
5 You .... Harry for the answer. I can tell you.
6 You look really tired. You studied all night last night, so tonight you .... so hard.
7 You .... yet! You haven't had anything to eat.
8 You .... my letters. They're private.
9 We .... yet. We've got plenty of time to get to the station.
10 I'm sure the shop won't be busy so you .... if you don't want to.

should

81 Make one sentence with **should** and one sentence with **shouldn't**.

1 GARY: I always feel tired these days. What do you think I should do?
   ANNE: *You should have* a holiday. *You shouldn't work* so hard.
2 GARY: I've got another hole in one of my teeth. What do you think I should do?
   ANNE: .... to the dentist. .... so many sweets.
3 GARY: I've got a terrible headache again. What do you think I should do?
   ANNE: .... an aspirin. .... without your glasses.
4 GARY: I've got a bad cough. What do you think I should do?
   ANNE: .... some medicine. .... so many cigarettes.
5 GARY: Bill wants to borrow my car for the weekend, but he's a terrible driver. What do you think I should do?
   ANNE: .... him that you need it. .... it to him.

82 You are asking a friend for advice. Make questions with **Do you think I / we should ...?**

1 There are two buttons missing on this shirt I've just bought.
   Do you think I should take it back to the shop?
2 I think I work very hard but I don't get a big salary.
   .... my boss for more money?
3 Simon's late again, and the train leaves in five minutes.
   .... a bit longer or go without him?
4 Martina has been sleeping for 18 hours and it's lunchtime soon.
   .... her up?
5 Jane is very nervous about going on holiday alone.
   .... with her?
6 We must be at the airport at 6.00 a.m. and the buses are not very good in the mornings.
   .... a taxi?
7 Burnt toast again! This toaster is getting worse.
   .... a new one?

47

83   What advice would you give in the following situations? Use **should**.

1   Alan had a terrible quarrel with his wife at the weekend. It was his fault.
What do you think he should do? I think _he should apologise to his wife._

2   Jane watches videos every night. She never goes out with her friends.
What advice do you give? I think ....

3   David and Paula haven't got much money. But they go out every night and spend money. At
the end of the month they can't pay their gas and electricity bills. What advice would you
give? I don't think ....

4   Joseph is very intelligent, but he wants to leave school and get a job. His parents think he
ought to go to university. What do you think?
I think ....

5   Maria told me some interesting news last night, but she said, 'Please don't tell anyone.' Now
Clare has asked me about Maria's news. What do you think I should do?
I don't think ....

I have to

84   Write questions using **… have to …** Look at the answers before you write the questions. Some of the
questions are in the present and some of them are in the past.

1   JOE: At school, I had to learn a lot of irregular verbs by heart. What
did you have to learn by heart?
CATH: The dates of all the kings and queens in history. It was boring!

2   JEAN: I really must go home. I have to get up early tomorrow.
LIZ: What about Chris? .... early tomorrow?
JEAN: No, he doesn't, so he can stay a bit longer.

3   BRIAN: I didn't pass my driving test first time. I had to take it three times. How many times
.... your driving test?
TOM: Only once. I passed first time.

4   PHIL: This book is so boring. I hope I finish reading it soon.
CAROL: Why .... it?
PHIL: Because I've got a literature exam next week.

5   NED: My mother wanted me to be a pianist. So for years I had to go to music lessons.
DIANA: What about your sister? .... to music lessons, too?
NED: No, she had to do ballet lessons.

6   SUE: I must be at work early tomorrow. I arrived at 10 o'clock this morning.
MEG: What time .... there normally?
SUE: 8.30!

85 Complete the sentences with the correct form of **have to**. Some of them are in the present and some of them are in the past. Use the verb in brackets ( ).

1 MARK: I don't like cabbage.
   SUE: That's OK. You can leave it. You _don't have to eat it._ (eat)

2 DAVE: We have to write a 1000–word essay before next Friday.
   JILL: What about me? .... one, too? (write)
   DAVE: Yes, I think so. Everybody has to do one.

3 PAUL: John's going to the bank later. He needs some money.
   MICK: He .... to the bank. I can lend him some. (go)

4 ANN: CAN YOU PASS ME THE SALT, PLEASE?
   PETE: You .... I'm not deaf! (shout)

5 PAT: Did Ruth enjoy her summer job in France?
   SAM: No, she hated it. She .... every day, so she wasn't able to see anything of the country. (work)

6 JOHN: Which job is Harry going to accept?
   RUTH: I don't know. He's going to think about it at the weekend. He
          .... today. (decide)

7 IAN: I really enjoyed Jane's party last night, but there were no buses home after midnight.
   LYNN: .... home? (walk)
   IAN: Yes, and it was a long way!

8 BETH: What's the matter with Tim?
   KATE: I'm not sure. The doctor says he .... in bed for a few days. (stay)

9 JOE: Was Tina angry when you told her the news?
   FRED: She already knew it so I .... her. (tell)

there ... and it ...   Units 36–38

86 Put in **there** or **it**.

1 MUM: _There's_ a good programme on TV tonight. _It's_ about computers.
   DAD: I'm not interested in computers. Is .... a long programme?
   MUM: No, only half an hour. Why?
   DAD: Because ....'s another programme I want to watch at 9.30.

2 JUAN: Excuse me. Is .... a bank near here?
   MARK: Yes, ...'s one on the corner of Broad Street.
   JUAN: Is .... open at lunchtime?
   MARK: Yes, I think so.

3 JANE: (*standing outside a restaurant*) This is the new Mexican restaurant.
   MARY: Is .... expensive?
   JANE: No, I don't think so. Look, ...'s an empty table. Let's go in.

4 DAVE: Mum, ... isn't any soap in the bathroom.
   MUM: Yes, ... is. ....'s a new packet on the shelf.
   DAVE: I can't see ....
   MUM: ....'s next to the shampoo.

87 You are on a tour of the National Museum. You're looking at paintings. Put in **there is / are / was / were / has been / will be**.

Welcome to the National Museum, ladies and gentlemen. We've only got one hour and
(1) ..*there is*.. a lot to see, so let's start.
On your left, you can see a painting by Rembrandt. (2) .... seven works by
Rembrandt here now. Last year (3) .... eight but sadly (4) .... a
robbery at the museum some months ago and the painting was stolen.
For those of you who are interested, (5) .... a major exhibition of Rembrandt's
work in London at the moment, and one next year in Amsterdam. I'm sure (6) ....
a lot of visitors to both exhibitions.
Now in this room, (7) .... a very famous painting by Picasso. And this painting on
the right is very interesting. It's by an Italian artist but we don't know which one. Oh no! It's
disappeared. (8) .... another robbery! Quick! Phone the police!

88 Put in **it/there + is(n't)/was(n't)**.

We had some interesting weather in the country yesterday. In Brightlea, (1) ..*there was*.. snow.
(2) .... unusual to have snow in the spring in this country. But last winter, when
everybody wanted to go skiing, (3) .... any snow at all.
Here in Wellbrough, the capital city, (4) .... windy yesterday. But that's normal.
(5) .... often a strong wind in spring. But (6) .... also very cold.
My sister lives in Stratton, on the east side of the country and she said that yesterday
(7) .... really dark in the middle of the afternoon and (8) .... a storm. It
frightened her children.
And today, (9) .... cloudy. (10) .... raining yet but I think it will soon.

Ask Martin questions about the weather in the town where he lives. Use **it** or **there**.

	YOU:	MARTIN:
11 (a lot of rain in spring?)	*Is there a lot of rain in spring?*	Yes, quite a lot.
12 (raining / at the moment?)	................................?	No.
13 (sunny / at the moment?)	................................?	Yes.
14 (any snow in winter?)	................................?	Sometimes.
15 (any snow / last winter?)	................................?	Yes, quite a lot.

I do / Have you? / So am I etc.
(auxiliary verbs)

Units 39–41

89 Use the information about Simon and David to complete the sentences. Begin each sentence with **'Simon …'**.

	SIMON:	DAVID:
1 Have you got a car?	no	yes
2 Are you interested in sport?	yes	no
3 Do you live in a town?	yes	no
4 Are you married?	no	yes
5 Have you got any brothers and sisters?	yes	no
6 Were you good at school?	yes	no
7 Did you study at university?	no	yes
8 Are you going on holiday this year?	yes	no
9 Have you visited many countries?	no	yes

1 Simon *hasn't got a car but David has.*
2 Simon *is interested in sport but David isn't.*
3 Simon ....
4 ....
5 ....
6 ....
7 ....
8 ....
9 ....

90 Write answers. Use **Do you?**, **Isn't it?**, etc.

1 I fell off my bike yesterday.	*Did you?*	Are you all right now?
2 I don't want to meet Jim.	....................?	Why not?
3 My husband can't cook at all.	....................?	What a pity.
4 Jane has lent me her laptop for tonight.	....................?	That's good of her.
5 You forgot to telephone me yesterday.	....................?	I'm sorry.
6 David doesn't use his car very much.	....................?	How does he get to work?
7 It hasn't rained for over two weeks.	....................?	That's very unusual.
8 I'm not going to eat chocolate anymore.	....................?	Are you on a diet?
9 I was ill yesterday.	....................?	What was the matter?
10 Your answer was wrong, I'm afraid.	....................?	What was the right answer?

91 Complete these sentences with a positive question tag (**is it?**, **can you?**, etc.) or a negative question tag (**weren't you?**, **hasn't it?**, etc.)

A: Now, you were born in Alaska, (1) *weren't you?*

B: Yes, that's right.

A: And then you all moved to New York, (2) ....?

B: Well, no. We moved to Los Angeles first, then to New York.

A: Sorry. But you don't live in New York now, (3) ....?

B: No, my family do, but I live in Washington.

A: I see. Now, you've got two brothers, (4) ....? And you are all actors. That's very unusual, (5) ....?

B: Yes, I think it is, but my parents were both actors, so …

A: They weren't very happy at first about you becoming an actor, (6) ....?

B: No, not at first. They didn't want me to follow in their footsteps. But now they're really pleased about my success.

A: I know you've acted with your brothers in a film but you haven't made a film with your parents yet, (7) ....?

B: No, but we are hoping to do one together next year.

A: That's very interesting. Tell me about it.

B: Well, it's about …

92 Mark has the same kind of job as Sandra. Write what Mark says. Use **too** or **either**.

SANDRA

1 I work in a hotel.
2 I can't speak a foreign language.
3 My manager is very good.
4 I haven't got any friends at work.
5 I don't work at the weekends.
6 I started work last year.
7 I'm bored with my job.
8 My salary isn't very good.

MARK

I do too.
I can't either.
Mine ...
....
....
....
....
....

93   Read this information about John and Mary. Use **So ... Mary** (e.g. **So does Mary**.), **Neither ... Mary** (e.g. **Neither can Mary**.) or **Mary ...** (e.g. **Mary wouldn't**.).

JOHN		MARY		
likes comedy films		same	1	*So does Mary.*
would love to go to America		different	2	*Mary wouldn't.*
can't play tennis very well		same	3	*Neither ...*
isn't married		same	4	
doesn't like jazz music very much		different	5	
hasn't got any brothers		same	6	
is looking for a new job		different	7	
went to university		same	8	
never goes to discos		same	9	
will be 22 next birthday		same	10	

☺   And you? Write true answers about yourself where you are the same as Mary or John. Use **so ... I** or **neither ... I**.

Mary likes comedy films and so do I.
John can't play tennis very well and neither can I.

....

....

....

---

isn't/haven't/don't etc. (negatives)   Unit 42

94   Complete these sentences with a verb in the negative form.

1   William and Eve *didn't go* (not / go) to the cinema last night.
2   I'm hungry. I .... (not / have) dinner yet.
3   Sarah .... (not / do) her shopping during the week. She always does it on Saturdays.
4   Please .... (not / watch me) when I'm cooking. I .... (not / like) it.
5   I .... (not / read) the newspaper at the moment. You can borrow it.
6   You .... (not / come) and see me yesterday.
7   These flowers .... (not / look) good on the table. Put them on the TV.
8   It .... (not / rain) at the moment. We can go out.
9   Let's take Sally to the Chinese restaurant. She .... (not / eat) Chinese food before.

95 Martha is listening to Madame Petra. She is talking about Martha and her life. Unfortunately, a lot of it
is wrong.

> I think your name begins with an 'A', maybe Andrea or Angela. You
> were born in England but you lived in Germany when you were younger.
> You can speak four languages.
>
> You're married and you've got two children. Your husband is a scientist,
> I think. Your parents live in your house with you and your family.
>
> Your son's birthday is in June. He's a teenager and he will be 14 next
> June. You're going to buy him a new bicycle and a new camera for his
> birthday. You are very happy with your family and I think you would like
> to have two or more children.

Martha tells her where she is wrong. Complete her sentences with a verb in the negative form.

Martha says:
You're wrong about me.

1 My name _isn't Andrea._ It's Martha.
2 I .... in England. I was born in Scotland.
3 I .... in Germany when I was younger. I lived in the USA.
4 I .... four languages. I can only speak two.
5 Yes, I'm married but I .... two children. I've got one, Tony.
6 My husband .... a scientist. He's a salesman.
7 My parents .... in my house. They live in their own house.
8 You're right, my son's birthday *is* in June, but next June he .... 14, he'll
   be 10.
9 Yes, I'm going to buy him a new bicycle but I .... him a new camera.
10 I am very happy with my family but I .... to have any more children.

questions

96 You are asking Jack some questions. Write the full questions.

YOU   JACK

1	(live?) ...*Where do you live?*...	In the middle of the town.
2	(do?) ....?	I'm a teacher.
3	(university?) ....?	Yes, I studied physics.
4	(married?) ....?	Yes, I am.
5	(meet / your wife?) ....?	At a wedding!
6	(any children?) ....?	Yes, a daughter called Emily.
7	(Emily / to school?) ....?	No, not yet. She's only three.
8	(your wife / work?) ....?	Yes, at home. She looks after Emily.
9	(enjoy your job?) ....?	Yes, most of the time.
10	(it / a difficult job?) ....?	Sometimes, but I like the children.
11	(weeks / holiday?) ....?	Twelve weeks a year.

97 Complete these subject and object questions. Use the verb in brackets ( ).

1 A: There are some beautiful flowers on the table.
   B: Who *put them* there? (put)

2 A: I went to the cinema last night.
   B: What *did you see?* (see)

3 A: Oh dear! I spent a lot of money yesterday.
   B: What ....? (buy)

4 A: We're all really hungry after our swim.
   B: OK. Who .... a sandwich? (want)

5 A: I'm going to explain to Meg why I can't see her again.
   B: What .... to her? (say)

6 A: Julia likes George but he doesn't really like her. Someone else does.
   B: Who .... Julia? (like)

7 A: I can hear music next door.
   B: Me too. Who .... the piano? (play)

8 A: ... and just at that moment, a man opened the window and started to climb out.
   B: What .... next? (happen)

9 A: Have you got a problem with the exercise, Maria?
   B: Yes. I don't understand this word. What ....? (mean)

55

98 Complete the questions. Each question ends with a preposition (**to/for/at/with**, etc.).

1 A: Jane's been talking on the telephone for hours.
   B: Who 's she talking to?

2 A: Jim has been waiting a long time.
   B: Who ....?

3 A: I wrote six letters yesterday.
   B: Who ....?

4 A: The new man in the Export Department is a Spanish speaker.
   B: Where ....?

5 A: Sarah doesn't live on her own. She shares her apartment.
   B: Who ....?

6 A: You really should read this book. It's a wonderful story.
   B: What ....?

7 A: Oxford is a very famous city.
   B: What ....?

8 A: We sold our car last week.
   B: Who ....?

9 A: Laura has been standing and looking out of the window for a long time.
   B: What ....?

99 Write questions with **which/what/how** + the word in brackets ( ).

1 A: We can catch the train if we hurry.
   B: _What time does it_ leave?   (time)

2 A: I'm learning Spanish, French and Arabic at the moment.
   B: _Which language do you_ prefer?   (language)

3 A: I'm really tired today. I went for a long walk yesterday.
   B: .... walk?   (far)

4 A: I've got dark hair but my sister's is completely different.
   B: .... her hair?   (colour)

5 A: Everyone thinks I'm younger than Tom because he's much taller than me.
   B: .... he?   (tall)

6 A: We must go. Are you ready?
   B: Nearly. .... wear – the black ones or the brown ones?   (shoes)

100 Find the mistakes and correct them.

1 What time leaves the train?   _What time does the train leave?_
2 Why you didn't ring me last night? ....?
3 To who are you giving that present? ....?
4 How much has spent Mary? ....?
5 Where did Jenny went for her holidays last year? ....?
6 What do you usually in the evenings? ....?
7 What did happen next? ....?
8 When was built the Taj Mahal? ....?

101 Complete the questions. Sometimes there is more than one possible question.

1 REBECCA: *Did you* enjoy your holiday?
  DENISE: Yes thanks, it was wonderful.
  REBECCA: Where ....?
  DENISE: To Jamaica.
  REBECCA: Who ....?
  DENISE: Two friends from my office.
  REBECCA: What ....?
  DENISE: It was sunny every day.

2 ROBERT: What ....?
  DANIEL: I've broken my arm.
  ROBERT: How ....?
  DANIEL: I fell off my bike.
  ROBERT: .... hurt?
  DANIEL: Not now, but it did.

3 LINDA: What ....?
  CLARE: I'm a teacher.
  LINDA: .... in a primary or a secondary school?
  CLARE: Secondary. My pupils are aged 14 to 16.
  LINDA: What ....?
  CLARE: Maths and physics.
  LINDA: How long ....?
  CLARE: Since 1988.

Do you know where ...?

102 Answer these questions with **I don't know** + the word in brackets ( ).

1 Is it Sue's birthday next week?
  (when) *I don't know when it is.*

2 Is she leaving because she's unhappy?
  (why) ....

3 Are John and Julia getting married this summer?
  (when) ....

4 Is that your new camera? It looks expensive. Did it cost a lot?
  (how much) ....

5 Did *Ann* tell you the news about Frank?
  (who) ....

6 Did John buy you a watch for your last birthday?
  (what) ....

103 Write questions with **Do you know where/when/what …**, etc.

1 You want to know the time of the first train to London tomorrow morning. Ask the person in the information office.
Do you know when the first train to London is tomorrow morning?

2 All the shops are closed today. You want to know why. Ask.
....?

3 You want to find the Regent Hotel. You ask a stranger in the street.
....?

4 Someone told you that John is going to leave his job. You want to know why.
....?

5 Someone told you that Mrs Smith, your old teacher, has died. You want to know when.
....?

104 Some words in this report are difficult to read. Ask questions to get the missing information. Use **Do you know …**

John Carter left home at (1) ▨▨▨▨▨▨ yesterday morning. He was wearing a (2) ▨▨▨▨▨▨ and a ▨▨▨▨▨▨ He wasn't alone. (3) ▨▨▨▨▨▨ was with him. First he went into a shop and bought a camera. It cost (4) ▨▨▨▨▨▨ Then he went into a (5) ▨▨▨▨▨▨ shop and came out carrying a long, thin package. The person with him was laughing, probably because (6) ▨▨▨▨▨▨ They walked to the station and caught the fast train which was going to (7) ▨▨▨▨▨▨ We know that journey usually takes (8) ▨▨▨▨▨▨ but yesterday it was much slower. My officers were at Dover station waiting for the two men but they were not on the train.

1 _Do you know what time he left home yesterday morning?_
2 ....
3 ....
4 ....
5 ....
6 ....
7 ....
8 ....

She said that … / He told me to … (reported speech)

105 Who is coming to the party on Saturday? Write sentences with **He/She said (that)** … or **He/She told me (that)** …

CAROLINE: I'm working really hard. I don't have time to go out in the evenings.

STEPHEN: I've got a few days' holiday. I'm going to Italy.

DAVE: I'm ill. I've been in bed for two days.

MARIA

TIM

ANNA: I don't like parties. I can't dance.

SUE: I love parties. I'll be free on Saturday.

MARIA: Did you invite Caroline to our party on Saturday?
TIM: Yes, but she can't come. She said (1) *she was working really hard* and (2) *she didn't have time to go out in the evenings.*
MARIA: OK. What about Stephen?
TIM: No. He said (3) .... and (4) ....
MARIA: Dave?
TIM: No. He said (5) .... and (6) ....
MARIA: Anna?
TIM: No, not Anna. She said (7) .... and (8) ....
MARIA: What about Sue?
TIM: Yes. She said (9) .... and (10) ....
MARIA: Good. That's a start!

106 Put in **say/said** or **tell/told**.

1 What did he *tell* you to do?
2 Lena .... that the banks were closed on Saturdays.
3 Have you .... him your news?
4 I think she .... she couldn't come to the party.
5 Jackie .... to me that she wanted to see you.
6 I .... him not to speak on the phone for too long.
7 Did Sam .... anything about me?
8 I didn't .... the teacher why I was late.

107 At the office. Jane's manager is looking for her. Read what these people say about her.

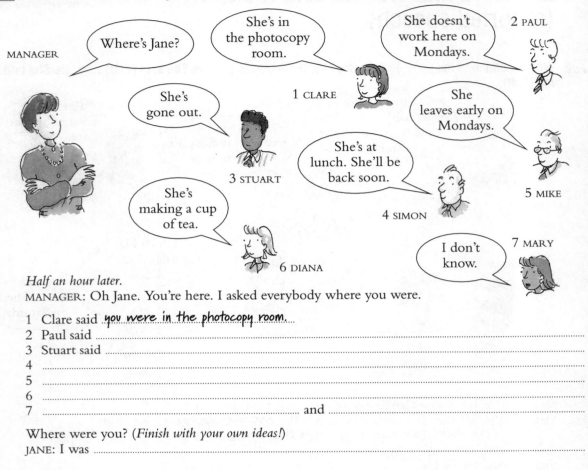

Half an hour later.
MANAGER: Oh Jane. You're here. I asked everybody where you were.

1 Clare said *you were in the photocopy room.*
2 Paul said ....
3 Stuart said ....
4 ....
5 ....
6 ....
7 .... and ....

Where were you? (*Finish with your own ideas!*)
JANE: I was ....

do / to do / doing

108 Choose the correct form of the verb.

1 Could I *borrow* your dictionary, please?
   to borrow / borrow / borrowing

2 I would like .... the President of our country.
   meet / meeting / to meet

3 Why is that car .... outside our house?
   stop / to stop / stopping

4 You don't look well. You should .... to bed.
   going / to go / go

5 Do we have .... now? I'm enjoying myself.
   to leave / leaving / leave

6 A: Shall I .... off the TV? B: Yes, please.
   turn / turning / to turn

7 Harry was .... out of the window when he heard a loud noise.
    look / to look / looking

8 We used .... a dog but it died last year.
    having / to have / have

9 A: When are you going .... John the news? B: Tonight, I think.
    tell / telling / to tell

10 I must .... some postcards this weekend.
    to write / writing / write

11 Sally says she wants .... a nurse when she's older.
    being / to be / be

12 You didn't need .... any more eggs. We had some in the fridge.
    buy / to buy / buying

109 Put the verb in the right form, using **to ...** or **-ing**.

Dear Sally

Thank you for your last letter. It was good to hear from you. My big news is that
I've decided (1) ...to change... (change) jobs. I finish (2) ...working. (work) at Simpsons next
month and start in my new company, Galt, the week after. Simpsons didn't want me
(3) .... (leave) but Galt offered me more money and more opportunities. I
hope (4) .... (be) a manager there in two years.

By the way, I forgot (5) .... (tell) you – I'm learning (6) ....
(drive). My new company offered (7) .... (let) me use one of their cars, which
was very good of them. I had a lot of problems at first because I wanted
(8) .... (do) everything quickly. My teacher thought I was a bit dangerous on
the road! He suggested (9) .... (slow) down, and now it's getting better.

I'm having a party on the 25th and would love (10) .... (see) you.

Perhaps you could persuade your brother (11) .... (come) with you as well.
I really enjoyed (12) .... (dance) with him at your party.

My neighbours have promised (13) .... (go) out for the evening, so we can
play the music as loud as we want.

I must stop (14) .... (write) now and do some work. See you on the 25th, I
hope.

Love
    Claire

110   Complete sentences with **advised/persuaded/let** etc. Use **to** if necessary.

1   The doctor said I should stop eating chocolate.
The doctor *advised me to stop eating chocolate.*   (advise)

2   I learnt to drive from my brother.
My brother .... (teach)

3   I said to David: 'Don't play with those matches.'
I .... (tell)

4   Stuart didn't allow his young sons to play with toy guns.
Stuart .... (let)

5   Jane didn't want to come swimming with us, but we asked her again and again and in the end she said, 'yes'.
We .... (persuade)

6   I was surprised that you married him.
I .... (expect)

7   My father said I had to pay back all the money I borrowed.
My father .... (make)

111   Finish each sentence with **(to) do something** or **(for) something**. Use your own ideas.

1   Tim went upstairs to *wash his hair.*
2   Jim went upstairs for *a book.*
3   I wrote to Mary to ....
4   Jane is going to ring the airport for ....
5   Let's open the window for ....
6   Mark turned on the TV to ....
7   Kevin is going to the kitchen ....
8   You need more money ....
9   Lucy hasn't got enough time ....
10   Jill waited a long time ....

112   Which ones are right? Sometimes only one sentence is right, sometimes two are right.

1   A: Why are you going to the post office?
B: a) To get some stamps.   *right*
      b) For getting some stamps.   *wrong*
      c) For some stamps.   *right*

2   a) Kate telephoned the station for asking about the London trains.   ....
    b) Kate telephoned the station to ask about the London trains.   ....
    c) Kate telephoned the station for information about the London trains.   ....

3   a) I'm waiting for the rain stopping.   ....
    b) I'm waiting for the rain to stop.   ....
    c) I'm waiting for the rain stop.   ....

4   a) We don't need much money to buy tickets.   ....
    b) We don't need much money for tickets.   ....
    c) We don't need much money for buy tickets.   ....

Review (do / to do / doing)

113 Complete these sentences with the verbs from the box. Put them in the right form using **to ...** or **-ing**.

~~swim~~	ask	speak	meet	answer
learn	shop	look for	~~go~~	wait

1 Would you like *to go* to the new Thai restaurant for dinner?
2 Everybody enjoyed *swimming* in the lake.
3 My younger brother is interested in .... to play tennis.
4 Why did you take my dictionary without .... me?
5 Kathy's mother asked her not .... on the telephone for too long.
6 James flew to San Francisco .... his American cousins for the first time.
7 Mike left his village .... a job in the city.
8 Pam closed the door before .... the phone.
9 Peter wanted us .... for him outside the bank.
10 Let's go .... in the city centre. I need a new pair of jeans.

114 Complete the sentences. Put the verbs in brackets ( ) in the correct form.

JIM: What are you doing this weekend?
PAT: Well on Saturday we're going (1) *swimming* (swim). Would you like (2) *to come* (come) with us?
JIM: I can't swim without someone (3) .... (hold) me. I've been thinking of (4) .... (have) lessons.
PAT: Well, I can help you. I taught Clive (5) .... (swim).
JIM: Did you? OK, I'll come on Saturday.

BEN: Oh dear! I'm not very good at (6) .... (cook).
ALAN: What are you trying (7) .... (make)?
BEN: A cheese souffle.
ALAN: Let me (8) .... (help) you.
BEN: No, it's OK thanks. I must (9) .... (learn).

JANE: What did you do after (10) .... (finish) school?
ROB: I studied law. My father is a lawyer and he persuaded me (11) .... (go) to law school.
JANE: Did you enjoy it?
ROB: Not really, because it wasn't my choice. My father made me (12) .... (do) it. I wanted (13) .... (be) a journalist.
JANE: So what happened?
ROB: After two years of law school I left without (14) .... (tell) my father, and went (15) .... (live) in France.
JANE: And now you work for a French newspaper in London.
ROB: Yes, that's right.

I/me/my/mine/myself etc.

115 Complete the sentences. Use **I/she/they** etc. and **us/him/you** etc.

1 He likes Jane but ..*she doesn't like him.*..
2 We're looking at Mr and Mrs Warner but _____
3 She wants to talk to me but _____
4 Jo and Mary often write to you but _____
5 I want to meet him but _____
6 You can telephone us but _____
7 He visits his grandparents but _____

116 Put in **my/your/his/its** etc.

1 Did you enjoy ..*your*.. holiday?
2 I forgot _____ umbrella this morning so I got wet.
3 When are we moving to _____ new house?
4 The neighbours are angry because someone stole _____ car last night.
5 Sydney is famous for _____ opera house.
6 Oliver's got two sisters. _____ older sister is married.
7 The lion lifted _____ head and looked at us.
8 Jill had a wonderful time. It was the best holiday of _____ life.
9 My husband gave me _____ grandmother's ring when we got married.
10 I'm sorry I didn't telephone you. I lost _____ number.

117 Complete the letter. Use **I/you/he** etc. or **her/him/them** etc. or **our/your/their** etc. or **mine/his** etc.

> *Dear Laura*
> *Thank you for (1) your letter. It was good to hear from (2) you and to know*
> *(3) _____ news.*
> *Let (4) _____ tell you my news. In June, (5) _____ sister, Sue, is getting*
> *married to John. Do you remember? I met John ten years ago, so he's an old friend of*
> *(6) _____. (7) _____ are getting married in the afternoon and my parents are*
> *having a big party for (8) _____ in the evening. (9) _____ am really happy for*
> *her, and for John. After the wedding they are coming to stay with (10) _____*
> *because they haven't got a house yet. So we will all be one big, happy family.*
> *My brother, Kevin, is taking (11) _____ final examinations next month. After*
> *that (12) _____ wants to get a job in a hospital. I think it will be difficult for*
> *(13) _____ but he really wants to be a doctor. Good luck to (14) _____!*
> *Last week I met Jane and Christina Sarton. Do you remember (15) _____?*
> *(16) _____ brother was at school with us. I gave Jane your telephone number and she*
> *gave me (17) _____. Perhaps we can all meet sometime soon.*
> *I must stop now. By the way, I found a silver pen in my room. It's not*
> *(18) _____. Is it (19) _____? I know you've got a silver one.*
> *My parents send (20) _____ love to you and (21) _____ parents.*
> *Love*
> *Wendy*

118 Complete the sentences. Use **himself/themselves** etc. or **by myself / by herself** etc. or **each other**.

1 He was very surprised when he looked at ..himself... in the mirror.
2 I don't like going to the cinema with other people. I prefer going ..by myself..
3 Joseph loves Christina and Christina loves Joseph. They love ..each other...
4 The child had no brothers or sisters, so she often had to play ....
5 My husband and I lived in the same street when we were children, so we saw .... very often.
6 A: Are you talking to me?
  B: No, I'm talking to ....!
7 Paul and Mike have known .... for 10 years.

Continue in the same way. Use the verbs in the box.

| wrote | cut | ~~lived~~ | understand | enjoyed | went |

8 Charles ..lived by himself... in a large house by the sea.
9 I'm afraid that the children are going to .... on the broken glass.
10 Marie speaks only French and Jill speaks only English so they can't ....
11 She didn't go to Madrid with anyone. She ....
12 We had a great time in London together. We really ....
13 Marianne and Catherine were pen friends for a long time. They .... to .... every week for 5 years.

119 What's wrong? Re-write the sentences correctly. One sentence is correct.

1 Is this book your? _Is this book yours?_
2 Meg and I have known us for five years. _Meg and I have known each other for five years._
3 James gave me those books. I really like it. ....
4 Some friends of them told them the news. ....
5 Patty gave her brother a cassette and he gave she a video. ....
6 My brother and his wife are not happy together. They don't love themselves any more. ....
7 John is a good friend of me. ....
8 It's your decision, not ours. ....
9 I like this house but her windows are broken. ....
10 I know Mary but I don't know his brother. ....
11 I sometimes ask me why I work in a noisy, dirty city. ....

-'s (**Ann's camera**) etc.

120 Complete the sentences. Use **-'s** or **-s'** + a noun.

1 David and Sue are husband and wife. David is .....Sue's husband......
2 This car belongs to Ann. It's ....
3 The king lives in a very beautiful palace. The .... is very beautiful.
4 I was with Elena at her house last night. I was at .... last night.
5 All the students have put their books on the table. All .... are on the table.
6 My sister was born on 28th June. The 28th June is ....
7 Mrs Penn makes delicious cakes. .... are delicious.
8 My grandparents have a house next door to us. My .... is next door to ours.
9 Mr and Mrs Smith have a daughter, Chris. Mr and Mrs Smith are ....

121 This is Mike and Alan's room. Whose are the objects in the room – Mike's or Alan's?

Mike likes: football, motorbikes, chocolate, wild animals.
Alan likes: reading, playing the guitar, computer games, running.

1 ..The elephant poster is Mike's...........   5 ....
2 ....   6 ....
3 ....   7 ....
4 ....   8 ....

122 Complete the sentences. Use **-'s** / **-s'** / **the ... of ....**

1 What's ..the name of this street?..   (the name / this street)
2 When's ..Alice's birthday?..   (the birthday / Alice)
3 Which is .... ?   (the favourite team / John)
4 When's .... ?   (the end / the programme)
5 When's .... ?   (the anniversary party / your parents)
6 How big are .... ?   (the windows / the house)
7 What's .... ?   (the telephone number / the station)
8 Do you know .... ?   (the daughter / Mr Turner)
9 Did you go to .... ?   (the wedding / your aunt)

a/some; countable/uncountable

123 Write the opposites. Use **a** or **an**.

1 a big house
   a small house
2 a full glass
   ....
3 an easy question
   ....

4 a new book
   ....
5 a cold day
   ....
6 an expensive hotel
   ....

7 an old man
   ....
8 a light bag
   ....

124 Correct the spelling of these plurals.

1 ~~watchs~~   _watches_
2 knifes   ....
3 tomatos   ....
4 monkies   ....
5 babys   ....

Write the correct plural.

6 ~~foots~~   _feet_
7 childs   ....
8 tooths   ....
9 womans   ....
10 sheeps   ....

125 Complete the sentences. Put in **a/an/some** if necessary + words from the box.

| beautiful weather | | bad news | fruit | ~~long hair~~ | information |
| work | perfume | paper | new socks | new job | envelope |

1 Mary's got _long hair_ which comes half-way down her back.
2 There's .... about English courses in this book. It's quite useful.
3 I've got a card for Ian's birthday but I haven't got .... to put it in.
4 My daughter bought me .... for my birthday. It smells lovely.
5 I don't usually buy ...., but I did this morning. There was an interesting story in it.
6 A: Why is Jane crying? B: She's just had ....
7 Oh dear! Look at this hole! I need ....
8 It's .... today, isn't it? Let's go swimming.
9 I'm sure you've all got .... to do, so please be quiet and do it!
10 Julia is really happy. She's got .... in a multi-national company. It's a big change from her old one.
11 Please eat .... I bought a lot in the market today.

126 The Campbell family are packing their suitcases for their summer holiday. Here are some things they are taking with them.

1 JOHN

2 SARAH

3 MRS CAMPBELL

4 MR CAMPBELL

Complete the sentences. Use **a(n)** / **some** / **a (two) pair(s) of ...** for each person.

1 John is taking
  two pairs of shorts
  a hat
  some towels
  some suntan oil

2 Sarah is taking
  ....
  ....
  ....
  ....

3 Mrs Campbell is taking
  ....
  ....
  ....
  ....

4 Mr Campbell is taking
  ....
  ....
  ....
  ....

☺ And you? Next month, you are going on holiday for three weeks to Australia (or the mountains of Switzerland, or Florida). Write six things that you are going to take with you.

I'm going to take
1 ....   4 ....
2 ....   5 ....
3 ....   6 ....

a/an and **the**

127 Put in **a/an** or **the**.

1 William wrote ..a... letter to his bank yesterday but he forgot to post it.
This morning, he saw ...the... letter on the kitchen table.
2 .... first bus in the morning leaves at 5.30 a.m.
3 When Eva White was younger she wanted to be .... musician. Now many people think
she is .... best trumpet-player in the world.
4 I've got .... idea. Let's go to .... new Greek restaurant in Main Street tonight.
5 Julia arrived at .... station at 7 o'clock and took .... taxi to .... city centre.
6 We usually eat our meals in .... kitchen. But if we have .... guest, we eat in
.... dining room.
7 Bern is .... capital of Switzerland. It's .... small city with about 133,000
inhabitants.
8 My office is on .... third floor of .... old building.
9 Martin lives in .... large town in .... middle of Germany but he wants to live in
.... country. He has got .... dog and he would like to take .... dog for long
walks.
10 Pat watched .... science fiction movie on TV last night. .... beginning of ....
film was fantastic but .... end was terrible.
11 I've known my husband, Sam, since I was six. We lived in .... same street when we
were children. Sam had .... older brother, Frank. I thought he was .... most
handsome boy in the world!
12 A: Excuse me, where's .... nearest bookshop?
B: It's at .... end of this street, on .... left. There's .... bus-stop in front of it.

128 Read the following story. There is a word missing in some lines. Put in **a(n)** or **the** where necessary.
Some of the lines are right.

Last night, moon was shining brightly. Clare's train	(1) _the moon_
arrived at the station and she got off. She went up	(2) _right_
to station manager and asked 'Do you know if there	(3) ....
is Italian restaurant near here?' 'Yes, it's very	(4) ....
near, just about 200 metres on left, opposite	(5) ....
Information Centre.' 'Thank you,' said Clare and	(6) ....
she started walking. She found restaurant and went	(7) ....
inside. There was woman playing the piano, and	(8) ....
there, in the corner of the room next to kitchen, was	(9) ....
Ron Allen – just man she wanted to see. He was	(10) ....
eating dinner, but when he saw Clare he stopped.	(11) ....
He thought she looked exactly same – beautiful and	(12) ....
calm. 'Have you got papers?' he asked. 'No, I haven't.	(13) ....
I've given them to police,' she replied. 'I hope they	(14) ....
will arrest you and send you to prison.' When he heard	(15) ....
her words, Ron jumped up, took knife from the table	(16) ....
and ran out. But outside …	

129 Complete the sentences with the words in brackets ( ). Use **the** where necessary.

1 Martin enjoys listening to ..music.. but he doesn't really like ..the music.. that his son plays on his guitar.   (music)

2 .... is one of my favourite sports.   (football)

3 Joe wasn't interested in .... when he was at school but he's just read a book about .... of the South American Indians and he really enjoyed it.   (history)

4 I must show you .... of our holiday in Ireland. Pat's really very good at taking ....   (photos)

5 .... opposite my house blew down in the wind last night. I don't think it's a good idea to have .... near houses.   (trees)

6 Sarah loves .... When she visits foreign countries, she always goes to local restaurants and tries .... which is typical of that region.   (food)

7 A: What's good on the menu today?
   B: .... is excellent.
   A: I'm afraid I don't eat ....   (chicken)

8 David spends a lot of time travelling on business. He enjoys staying in ....   (hotels)

9 A: Did Chloe return .... she borrowed from you last week?
   B: Yes. I told her, 'I need it back. .... doesn't grow on trees!'   (money)

130

A Here is some information about a famous river. Put in **the** where necessary.

(1) ..The.. Amazon is in (2) .... South America. It begins near (3) .... west of the continent, 160 kms from (4) .... Pacific Ocean. It starts in (5) .... Andes in (6) .... Peru and then it flows through (7) .... Brazil and out into (8) .... Atlantic.

B Now read about London. Put in **the** where necessary before the names of the famous places.

Most people want to see where the Queen lives when they visit (9) ..—.. London, so (10) .... Buckingham Palace is very popular. But I think the best thing to do is to take a boat trip on (11) .... River Thames to see all the famous buildings. You can get on the boat at (12) .... Westminster Bridge, near (13) .... Houses of Parliament. If you go down the river to (14) .... Tower of London, you will pass (15) .... St Paul's Cathedral on the way. This is a very old and beautiful church, and my favourite building.
As a change from sightseeing, you could go shopping along (16) .... Oxford Street, or maybe if you like animals, go to (17) .... London Zoo.
There's a lot to do and see in the capital. Come and see!

☺ And in your country?

What's the capital city? ....
Name one important street in your capital. ....
What's the most famous building? ....
What's your favourite building? ....
What's the name of the building that your government works in? ....

some and any

131 Put in **some** or **any**.

DAN: Let's go for a picnic by the river tomorrow.
RUTH: OK. We'll make (1) ..*Some*.. sandwiches. What do we need?
DAN: We haven't got (2) .... bread. Can you buy (3) ....?
RUTH: Yes, sure. What about butter?
DAN: We've got (4) .... I'll buy (5) .... cheese.
RUTH: OK, and is there (6) .... orange juice in the fridge?
DAN: No, I'll get (7) ....
RUTH: Good. Do we need (8) .... apples or cherries?
DAN: Just (9) .... apples.
RUTH: Oh dear! I haven't got (10) .... money to buy the bread!
DAN: Don't worry. I'll lend you (11) ....

132 Complete these sentences. Use **some** or **any** + a suitable noun.

1 Leo has gone to the bank to get ..*some money.*...
2 Can I have .... in my tea? I don't like it black.
3 I'd like .... about hotels in London, please.
4 I want to light the barbecue but I haven't got ....
5 Clare is not very happy with her maths exam. She knows she made ....
6 Can I borrow ....? I need to wash my hair.
7 Sorry, but everyone has to sit on the floor. We haven't got .... yet.
8 There wasn't .... in my village last winter so we couldn't go skiing.
9 Can I have .... on my bread? I prefer strawberry if you have it.

133 Put in **somebody** (or **someone**) / **something** / **anybody** (or **anyone**) / **anything**.

1 I feel a bit sick. I think I've eaten ..*something*... bad.
2 Did .... telephone me last night?
3 A: What's the matter? B: I think there's .... in the garden.
4 A: What's wrong? B: I've put .... in my coffee, and it wasn't sugar!
5 Please don't tell .... about the letter. It's a secret.
6 You look bored. Would you like .... to do?
7 Has .... seen my bicycle? It's not in the garage.
8 There isn't .... to watch on TV tonight. Let's go out.
9 .... dropped a £10 note in the street outside my house yesterday.
10 I don't think I've learnt .... from his lecture.

some/any/no/none

Units 75–76

134 Re-write these sentences. Use **any** or **no**.

1 There isn't any milk in the fridge. *There's no milk in the fridge.*
2 We had no electricity last night. *We didn't have any electricity last night.*
3 I haven't got any grandparents. ....
4 There's no time to visit the museums. ....
5 We didn't have any rain in July last year. ....
6 There are no clouds in the sky today. ....
7 There was no sugar in my tea. ....
8 Tim hasn't got any books in his house. ....

135 Right or wrong? Correct the underlined word where necessary. Use **some/any/no/none**. Three sentences are right.

1 Mary hasn't got <u>some</u> stamps in her purse. ...*any*...
2 There aren't <u>no</u> easy questions. ....
3 A: How many books did you read on holiday? B: <u>None</u>. ....
4 Would you like <u>some</u> ice-cream? ....
5 Please don't offer me any chocolates. I don't want <u>none</u>. ....
6 I didn't give him <u>no</u> money. ....
7 Have you written <u>any</u> postcards yet? ....
8 There are <u>any</u> biscuits in the tin. We must buy some. ....
9 Can I have <u>any</u> potatoes, please? ....

136 Complete the conversation between Jenny and her friend, Martin. Use **some/any/no/none**.

JENNY: Hi, Martin. How are you?
MARTIN: Fine, but busy. We've got (1) ...*some*... exams next week – remember?
JENNY: I know. How much work did you do last night?
MARTIN: (2) ...., I went to the cinema. What about you?
JENNY: I had (3) .... time last night. It was my sister's birthday so we all went out for dinner.
MARTIN: Have you done (4) .... work this morning?
JENNY: (5) ...., but not a lot. Anyway, I rang to ask you something. Do you know where my physics book is?
MARTIN: I've got (6) .... idea, but you can borrow mine if you want.
JENNY: Thanks.
MARTIN: Let's meet outside Natbank in the High Street this lunchtime. I need to get (7) .... money and I'll bring my physics book for you.
JENNY: Good idea. I'm very worried about the physics exam. Have you got (8) .... old exam papers? I'd really like to look at them.
MARTIN: I haven't got (9) .... but my brother's got (10) .... from 1995. I'll bring them with me at lunchtime.
JENNY: Wonderful! See you at 12.30. OK?

somebody/anything/nowhere etc.

137 Put in **anybody (anyone)** / **anything** / **nobody (no-one)** / **nothing**.

1 There was a thunderstorm during the night but I heard ...*nothing*.....
2 There isn't .... I like on the menu.
3 Fred isn't a nice person. .... likes him.
4 I can't hear .... Can you turn the radio up?
5 Sheila's lonely in London because she doesn't know ....
6 What's that in your hand? ....
7 I haven't bought .... for Sarah's birthday.
8 .... can help you. You must do it yourself.
9 A: What are you doing tonight? B: ....
10 Ken was in hospital for two days but .... went to see him.
11 There wasn't .... in the cinema. It was completely empty.

138 Put in **somebody/anything/nowhere** etc.

Dear Phil
I've been here for two months and I don't like this place. I haven't met (1) ..*anybody*...... interesting. Also, it's very quiet in the evenings. All the shops and restaurants close early and the streets are empty. There's (2) .... to go and there is (3) .... good on TV.
    Then yesterday (4) .... told me about a sports club (5) .... near my house. So I decided to try it. I found it – it's only ten minutes from my house and it's great. There's weight-training, tennis, a swimming pool, and the people there are very friendly. (6) .... tells you what to do – you can choose for yourself. In the middle of the evening, (7) .... said, 'Hello, I'm Tony. Are you doing (8) .... later this evening? Would you like to go for (9) .... to eat?' I said, 'Yes, I'd love to.'
    We had delicious pizzas and that night I thought to myself, 'This town is getting better! I haven't been (10) .... for two months and now I've been to two new places in one evening and made a friend.'
    All the best
    Geoffrey

139 Complete the sentences. Use **somebody/anything/nowhere** etc. + **to ...** (e.g. **to go / to stay / to eat**).

SUE: I'm hungry.
DAD: Would you like (1) _something to eat?_
SUE: Yes, please.

FRED: I'm bored. I've got (2) ....
MUM: Go and play tennis.
FRED: All my friends are on holiday so I haven't got (3) .... with.

KEN: Let's have lunch in this restaurant.
MEG: It looks very busy. Is there (4) .... ?
KEN: Yes, there are two seats over there.

LIZ: We're going to Rome in September.
TIM: Wonderful.
LIZ: Yes, but we've got a problem. We haven't got (5) .... yet.
TIM: Have you tried The Plaza Hotel? They usually have free rooms.

PAM: I'm going to a really important party at the weekend and I need
        (6) ....
CAROL: You can borrow my new black dress if you want.

TANYA: Jerry, go and talk to Annie. She's in the kitchen.
JERRY: I haven't got (7) ....
TANYA: Of course you have! You always have lots to say. Go and talk about food or sport.

---

every and **all**

140 Complete the sentences with **every** + the correct form of the verb.

1 There are no losers in our competition. _Every_ child _wins_ (win) a prize.
2 When I was at school, ... teacher .... (be) female.
3 .... mountain in the Himalayas .... (be) over 3,000 metres.
4 .... car in our showroom .... (have) got a sun-roof, radio-cassette and electric windows.
5 I loved going to my grandparents' house when they were alive. .... room .... (be) filled with beautiful furniture.

141 Complete the sentences with **every/all** + the word in brackets ( ).

(morning)
1 It was raining yesterday, so I wrote letters _all morning._
2 .... I catch the number 91 bus to the supermarket.
3 Jane waited .... for the electrician to arrive. He came at 2.30 p.m.

(summer)
4 When I was a child, my family and I went to the same place for holidays ....
5 This year the weather has been terrible. I don't think we've seen the sun ....
6 David has got exams in the autumn so he'll have to study ....

(night)

7 .... last week Kate had the same dream.

8 My neighbours had a party on Saturday. The noise was terrible and I was awake
....

9 A: Why are you so tired this morning? B: I didn't go to bed. I worked ....

(day)

10 I want to keep fit so I try to go jogging ....

11 I'm really hungry. I haven't eaten ....

12 Jack doesn't go to the office .... Some days he works at home.

142 Put in **everybody** (or **everyone**) / **everywhere** / **everything** + a verb.

1 A: These shirts are expensive.
  B: _Everything is_ expensive in this shop.

2 A: Why are so many people wearing black?
  B: Because it's fashionable. .... wearing black this year.

3 A: Do you always watch ice-hockey on TV?
  B: Yes, ... in my family .... it. We love it.

4 A: Did you enjoy your day in London?
  B: Yes, very much, but .... really busy because it was school holiday
  time.

5 A: My grandfather says that family life was better when he was young.
  B: Yes, a lot of old people think that .... better in the past.

6 A: Things in our country seem to be changing quickly at the moment.
  B: Well, it's not only our country. .... changing.

all/most/some/any/no/none   Unit 80

143 Complete the sentences. Use the word in brackets ( ). Sometimes you need **of** (**some of** / **none of** etc.).

1 My children were quiet _all_ the time I was at the dentist.   (all)

2 .... the passengers got off the bus in the city centre.   (most)

3 .... these books are not yours. You must take them back to the library.   (some)

4 I haven't read .... books by Agatha Christie.   (any)

5 .... these papers must leave this room. They're secret.   (none)

6 I think .... children like ice-cream, don't they?   (all)

7 You can buy .... the things you want in our local supermarket.   (most)

8 .... sportsmen and women receive a lot of money.   (some)

9 .... Jack's friends came to see him when he was ill.   (none)

10 When my father was young, there were .... cinemas in the town.   (no)

11 Linda has got some strange friends. I don't really like .... them.   (any)

12 My grandfather lived in the same house .... his life.   (all)

144 Write sentences. Use **all/most/some/none**.

> Richard is 40 years old. He's a manager in a large multi-national company. He and the people who work in his company answered some questions about their health.
>
> | | **Yes** |
> |------------------------------|---------|
> | Do you take regular exercise? | 63% |
> | Do you walk to work? | 25% |
> | Have you got a car? | 100% |
> | Do you use your car every day? | 80% |

1 *Most of Richard's colleagues take regular exercise.*
2 ....
3 ....
4 ....

> Lisa is 16 years old and she's a high school student. Read the answers that she and her friends gave to some different questions.
>
> | | **Yes** |
> |---------------------------------|---------|
> | Do you go to the cinema every month? | 37% |
> | Do you play some kind of sport? | 100% |
> | Do you study every night? | 0% |
> | Do you enjoy dancing? | 67% |

5 ....
6 ....
7 ....
8 ....

145 Write answers to these questions. Choose from **all/most/some/none** + **of it** / **of them**.

1 How many exercises in this book have you done?   *Some of them.*
2 How much of your work/study do you enjoy? ....
3 How many of the people in your street do you know? ....
4 How many houses in your street have got gardens? ....
5 How many families living near you have got young children? ....
6 How much of today's newspaper have you read? ....
7 How much of this exercise do you think you've done correctly? ....

both/either/neither

146 Put in **both/either/neither**. Use **of** where necessary.

1 A: Do you like pop music or jazz.
   B: I don't like *either of* them. I prefer classical music.

2 A: Jill looks tired.
   B: Yes, *both* her children are in bed ill.

3 A: Where would you like to go for your holidays this year? Greece or Spain?
   B: .... is fine with me. I like them both.

4 A: Which question did you answer, number 1 or number 3?
   B: .... I answered number 4.

5 A: Why's Jane in hospital?
   B: She had an accident yesterday and broke .... her legs.

6   A: Would you like potatoes or rice with your chicken?
    B: ...., please! I'm really hungry.

7   A: I enjoyed both those films.
    B: Did you? I didn't like .... them.

8   A: Did you know Jimmy or John when you were younger?
    B: They lived in the same street as me so I knew .... them.

9   A: Hurry up! We're going to be late. What's the problem?
    B: .... these shirts is the right colour. I need a blue one.

10   A: Have you read the latest two postcards from Mary in the States?
     B: No, I haven't read .... them, yet.

---

147   Write sentences about yourself and one of your friends. Think of some things which are similar in your lives. Use **Both of us / Neither of us ...**.

1   _Both of us live in apartments._
2   _Neither of us has (got) a dog._
☺   3   6   ....
    4   7   ....
    5   8   ....

---

a lot / much / many; (a) little / (a) few   **Units 82–83**

148   Look at the picture and see what is left after the wedding party is finished. Write sentences.
Use: **There aren't many ... / There isn't much ... / There isn't/aren't any ...**.

1   _There isn't much champagne._   5   ....
2   6   ....
3   7   ....
4   ....

149 Liz is asking you some questions. Write questions with **How much/many ...?** Then write your own answers. Use **a lot / not (very) much / not (very) many / a few / a little / none**.

1 LIZ: (books / be / on your table?) *How many books are there on your table?*
  YOU: *Not many.*

2 LIZ: (milk / you / like / in your coffee?) ....?
  YOU: ....

3 LIZ: (cars / you / see / out of the window?) ....?
  YOU: ....

4 LIZ: (money / you / spend / in one month?) ....?
  YOU: ....

5 LIZ: (good friends / you / have?) ....?
  YOU: ....

6 LIZ: (football / you / play?) ....?
  YOU: ....

7 LIZ: (pairs of socks / you / have?) ....?
  YOU: ....

8 LIZ: (fruit / you / eat / every day?) ....?
  YOU: ....

9 LIZ: (water / you / drink / every day?) ....?
  YOU: ....

150 Complete the text about Antarctica. Put in **little / a little**, **few / a few**.

Antarctica is a snow-covered continent. The average temperature at the South Pole is –51°C. (1) *Few* plants or animals can live on the land – it is too cold for them. The animal life is found on and in the sea. There are (2) .... scientists from different countries who live and work on special bases in Antarctica. On midsummer's day (December 22nd) there is daylight for 24 hours and so during this period (3) .... tourist ships and planes come to see this strange land. But in the winter there is (4) .... daylight for months. It must be a terrible place during the winter. The snow is always there – winter and summer – but in fact (5) .... snow falls in the year (an average of 12 – 20 cm). People say that it can be a beautiful place. At first, it appears frightening but after (6) .... time, some people fall in love with it.

old, nice etc. (adjectives); quickly, badly etc. (adverbs)

151 Complete the story about Jane's visit to China. Use the adjectives from the box + a suitable noun.

delicious	~~long~~	famous	old	big	difficult	friendly	hot	busy

Yesterday, Jane Greenwood flew back to London from China. It was a very (1) .long. flight. – 20 hours – and she feels tired today.

She was on holiday in China. She stayed in an (2) .... Three hundred years ago an emperor built it. The only problem was that there was no (3) .... in the rooms so everybody had cold showers. She visited many (4) ...., for example, The Great Wall of China. She ate some (5) .... Her favourite was egg fried rice. She met a lot of very (6) .... Jane can't speak Chinese so they spoke to her in English. She tried a few words in Chinese but people said it is a (7) .... to learn.

A lot of things in China surprised her. For example, the (8) .... There were hundreds and hundreds of bicycles on the roads all day and all night. There was never a quiet moment.

Jane wants to go back to China next year. She knows it is a (9) .... and she only saw a small part of it.

152 Complete the sentences with an adjective, an adverb or a noun.

1 John is sometimes a dangerous .driver. I think he drives .dangerously. when he's in a hurry.
2 Pam's old car was slow but her new one is very .fast.
3 James looked .... when his team won the game.
4 It rained .... all day yesterday and the ground was very wet.
5 Mmmmm, what a wonderful .... from the kitchen. What are you cooking? I'm sure it's going to taste ....
6 I think Mrs Burns is a good .... She taught my children ....
7 David hasn't got a lot of money so when he goes shopping he always looks .... at the prices.
8 My parents were hard .... They worked .... all their lives.
9 Jackie did .... in his test and had to take it again.
10 I spoke to Peter on the telephone this morning. He sounded really .... Someone stole his car yesterday.

153   Complete the conversation with **well** or **good**.

LAURA: You don't look very (1) _well_. Are you ill?
DIANA: No, I'm just a bit tired.
LAURA: Did you enjoy the party last night?
DIANA: Yes, it was very (2) .... Did you?
LAURA: Yes, very much. John plays the piano really (3) ...., doesn't he?
DIANA: Mmmm. I didn't know he was (4) .... at the piano.
LAURA: His sister's a (5) .... player too.
DIANA: Was she there last night?
LAURA: No, she wasn't feeling (6) ...., so she didn't come. I think she's got a bad cold.
DIANA: I don't remember her very (7) .... Was she at school with us?
LAURA: Yes, but she wasn't in the same class.
DIANA: You've got a (8) .... memory!

---

older/oldest (comparatives and superlatives)

154   Write sentences with **not as … as** and the comparative (**older / more difficult** etc.).

1   (Mexico City / London / expensive / crowded)
    Mexico City isn't as expensive as London but it is more crowded.

2   (city life / village life / friendly / exciting)
    ....

3   (motorways / country roads / interesting / fast)
    ....

4   (travelling by plane / travelling by bus / cheap / comfortable)
    ....

5   (Egypt / Iceland / green / warm)
    ....

6   (bicycles / cars / comfortable / easy to park)
    ....

155   Only two of these comparative sentences are correct. Correct the mistakes where necessary.

1   He got up more early than she did.   _He got up earlier than she did._
2   My computer is moderner than yours.   ....
3   Jack is a more good player than me.   ....
4   It's a bit hotter today.   ....
5   Is it more interesting as his last book?   ....
6   He paid less than you for the ticket.   ....
7   My mother is the same age like my father.   ....
8   Ann's headache is badder today.   ....
9   She lives much more far away now.   ....

156　Read the following comparison between the USA and Australia. Fill in the gaps with one word only.

> The USA has a much (1) ..bigger.. population
> (2) .... Australia, and American cities are
> (3) .... crowded than Australian ones.
>   There are not (4) .... many mountains in
> Australia (5) .... in the USA. Both countries
> have deserts and beautiful beaches. But America
> has many (6) .... rivers than Australia.
>   The northern and central parts of the USA
> have much (7) .... snow in winter than
> anywhere in Australia and generally these two
> areas have a (8) .... winter than Australia
> does. Australia is in the southern hemisphere
> and doesn't have its winter at the same time
> (9) .... countries in the northern
> hemisphere.
>   Most people in these countries speak the
> same language (10) .... each other – English
> – but their accents are very different. Some
> people say that the Americans are warmer and
> (11) .... friendly (12) .... the Australians
> but I don't see any difference.

☺　Now you write some sentences comparing your country with another country that you know. Use the paragraph about the USA and Australia to help you. Write about:

- the geography (rivers, mountains, cities, etc.)
- the weather (hot, wet, dry, cold, etc.)
- the people (language, character, etc.)

....

....

....

157　Comparing now and then. Albert is thinking about life today and life 40 years ago. Complete his sentences. Use **... than** or **not as ... as**.

1　(cars / fast)　　　　　　　*Cars are faster than they were.*
2　(children / more things)　　*Children have got more things than they had.*
3　(people / not work / hard)　*People don't work as hard as they did.*
4　(life / expensive)
5　(people / not / friendly)
6　(films / violent)
7　(people / live / long)
8　(house / good)
9　(families / not big)
10　(children / freedom)
11　(people / eat / good food)

158 Terry is asking you some questions about your life.
Write his questions. Use the superlative + the present perfect
(e.g. **the most beautiful … you've ever seen**).
Answer the questions in your own words.

1 TERRY: (What / good / holiday / you have?)
          What's the best holiday you've had?
    YOU: *My holiday in Greece last year.*

2 TERRY: (Who / interesting person / you / meet?)
          ....?
    YOU: ....

3 TERRY: (What / frightening experience / you / have?)
          ....?
    YOU: ....

4 TERRY: (What / bad film / you / see?)
          ....?
    YOU: ....

5 TERRY: (What / expensive thing / you / buy?)
          ....?
    YOU: ....

6 TERRY: (What / unusual food / you / eat?)
          ....?
    YOU: ....

7 TERRY: (Which / large city / you / go to?)
          ....?
    YOU: ....

8 TERRY: (What / useful present / you / receive?)
          ....?
    YOU: ....

---

enough and **too**

159 Complete the sentences. Use **enough** + one of the words from the box.

people	~~good~~	fit	~~money~~	plates	sweet	information	study

1 Have you got ..*enough money*.. to pay for all these things?
2 My English is not ..*good enough*.. for an interpreter's job.
3 We had 12 people for dinner last night but we didn't have ....!
4 Jane didn't pass her examination because she didn't ....
5 The party on Saturday was very quiet. There weren't .... there.
6 Is your tea ...., or would you like some more sugar?
7 I can't give you an answer because I haven't got ....
8 William couldn't run more than 200 metres because he wasn't ....

Now use **enough** + one of the words from the box + **to** (**do**, **eat**, **drive**, etc.).

money	~~old~~	well	time	sharp	warm

9 Mary is 14 years old. She isn't ..*old enough to drive*.. a car.
10 I can't use this knife. It's not .... the meat.
11 Oh dear! I haven't got .... Pete a birthday present. Can you lend me some?
12 You should stay in bed. You don't look .... to Tina's party.
13 That was a horrible test. Did you have .... all the questions?
14 It's only 13 degrees. It's not .... in the garden.

160 Complete the sentences. Use **too / too much / too many**.

1 Aunt Mary didn't buy the dress because it ..*was too*.. expensive.
2 Carl felt ill last night because he ..*had (or ate) too many*.. chocolates.
3 Jim doesn't use his bicycle in town because .... dangerous.
4 I didn't enjoy shopping in the market because there .... people.
5 We don't usually go to the beach at midday because it .... hot.
6 And he didn't sleep very well because he .... coffee.
7 I can't see anything because .... dark.
8 Ann doesn't like swimming in the sea because .... cold.

161 Peter lives in an old city which is very popular with tourists. He doesn't like it. Here are some of his reasons:

1 a lot of cars
2 very narrow streets
3 only 3 cinemas
4 a lot of noise and dirt
5 the parks are very small
6 very few things to do after work
7 a lot of tourists

Complete Peter's sentences. Use **too** or **enough**.

1 There are too many cars.
2 The streets are not wide enough. or The streets are too narrow.
3 There ....
4 There ....
5 The ....
6 There ....
7 There ....

☺ What about the place where you live? Are there some things you don't like? Use **too** and **enough** to write about your city / town / village.

....
....

162 When are you allowed to do certain things?

In Britain, at the age of:
   5 – You start primary school.
  12 – You can buy a pet (e.g. a dog or a cat).
  13 – You can work for two hours a day.
  16 – You can leave school.
       – You can get married with your parents' permission.
  17 – You can drive a car.
  18 – You can vote.
  21 – You can become a Member of Parliament.

Use the information to say whether these people are old enough to do what they want.
Use **too** or **enough**.

1 John is only 3 years old and he wants to go to school. Can he?
   No, he's too young to go to school.   or   *He's not old enough to go to school.*
2 My daughter is 14. Can she work in a shop after school?
   Yes, she's old enough to work for two hours a day.
3 Can Jane and Terry get married? They are 15.
   .... or ....
4 Can Peter start driving lessons? He's 17.
   ....
5 Barbara's 10 and she wants to buy a dog with her own money. Can she buy one?
   .... or ....
6 Eric is 16 and is fed up with school. Can he leave?
   ....
7 Ann is only 20 but she is very interested in politics and what is happening in her country. Can she become a Member of Parliament?
   .... or ....

Word order; still/yet/already   Units 92–94

163 Put the words in the right order where necessary. One sentence is right.

1 Rachel often is late for school.   *Rachel is often late for school.*
2 I already have won two tennis championships.   ....
3 Maria goes rarely to bed before midnight.   ....
4 My children? They are all adults now.   ....
5 My brother and I live still at home.   ....
6 When do you do usually your homework?   ....
7 I never can remember my car registration number.   ....
8 My sister sometimes is horrible to me.   ....
9 Clare speaks Spanish and she understands also Italian.   ....
10 John and Steve? They both are married now.   ....
11 My younger brother just has finished school.   ....

164 Complete the sentences. Use **still**.

1 It started snowing two hours ago and it is ...*still snowing*... heavily.
2 John bought an old car in 1990 and he .... today.
3 I know she said she was sorry, but I .... angry.
4 My father first went to a football game in 1975 and he .... every week.
5 I know you went swimming regularly when you were younger. Do you
   .... every day?
6 Monica felt ill two days ago and went to bed. She .... in bed.

165 Complete the sentences with the verb in brackets ( ). Use **still** (+ positive) and **yet** (+ negative).

1 TEACHER: OK everyone. Stop now. Please give me your test papers.
   STUDENT: Sorry, I *haven't finished yet.* (finish) *I am still writing.* (write)
2 A: Come on, we're going to be late.
   B: I .... keys. (look for)
   I .... (find)
3 Dear Sue
   The weather continues to be wet. It .... (rain)
   We .... (see the sun)
4 A: (*on the phone*) You sound very sleepy.
   B: Yes, I .... (get up)
   I .... bed. (be)
5 A: Are you and Tony friends again?
   B: No. He .... (apologise)
   I .... angry. (be)

at, until, before etc. (prepositions of time)   Units 96–98

166 Complete the sentences. Choose from the boxes.

at		night six weeks winter Thursday
on	+	midnight· 1900 Christmas 6.30 a.m.
in		~~evening~~ November 22nd 1963

1 After working all day, John is too tired to go out ...*in the evening.*...
2 Last night I went to bed ....
3 President Kennedy was shot ....
4 In Christian countries, most people don't work ....
5 Our cat stays out .... and comes back home in the morning.
6 Jill loves skiing so she usually takes her holidays sometime ....
7 My parents' alarm clock always rings ....
8 Her grandfather was born .... so he is now a very old man.
9 Mary is expecting a baby .... so she'll finish working soon.
10 I have a lecture .... so I can't meet you then, I'm afraid.

167 Complete the sentences with words from the box. In **one** sentence, no word is necessary.

at	on	in	until	since	for	from	to

1 Pat's uncle left Canada ..in.. 1968 and went to Brazil.
2 John is getting married .... the end of the month.
3 The accident happened .... Monday morning when Sue was driving to work.
4 Alan has been feeling sick .... he ate some fish last night.
5 Are you going to stay .... the end of the film?
6 The birds started singing .... half past four this morning.
7 We'll know the result of the exam .... three weeks.
8 An American player won the tennis championship .... Independence Day.
9 Robert is going to stop work .... next February.
10 I swim in the sea every day .... summer.
11 Does John really enjoy working .... night?
12 A: How long are you going to stay here? B: .... I can speak the language perfectly.
13 Kate went to Istanbul .... four days last spring.
14 Mark works hard .... Monday .... Friday, so he sleeps .... the weekend.

168 Complete the story of Jess Brewer's life. Use words from the box.

during	for	~~from~~	after	to	until	before	while	since

Jess Brewer was a pupil at her local school (1) ..from.. 1975 (2) .... 1988. (3) .... her last year at school she taught herself how to use computers, and this knowledge was very useful for her later. (4) .... leaving school, she went to university and studied mathematics. She was responsible for producing a student magazine on her computer (5) .... she was there. She stayed at university (6) .... four years and then decided to travel (7) .... finding a job.

She has been working as a computer programmer (8) .... she came back from her travels, but she wants to go away again. She knows that she has to stay with the computer company (9) .... she has enough money to go and do what she wants.

169 Jess is describing a normal day in her life. Complete her story. Use words from the box.

at	on	in	since	for	until	from
during	while	after	to	before		

I wake up (1) ..at.. about 7.30 a.m. (2) ..during.. the week, but much later (3) .... Saturdays. (4) .... I wake up, I move very fast. In fact, I'm very good (5) .... the mornings. I only need 20 minutes (6) .... the time my alarm clock rings (7) .... the time I leave the house. I don't have breakfast at home; I have to wait (8) .... I arrive at the office for a cup of coffee.

I start work (9) .... 9.00 a.m. and work (10) .... four hours. (11) .... lunchtime, I often sit in the park and read (12) .... I am eating my sandwiches. (13) .... going back to the office, I do some shopping. The afternoon passes very quickly. I work (14) .... 6 o'clock and then I go home. I've been working for the same company (15) .... 1994.

(16) .... the evenings, I usually watch TV or maybe go out for dinner with some friends. I don't go to bed late because I have to get up for work the next day. (17) .... the weekends, my routine is very different.

☺ Now write a paragraph about a normal day in your life. The following ideas will help you.

| wake up / get up? | work / school | afternoon? | bed? |
| breakfast? | lunchtime? | evenings? | |

I usually wake up ....

....

in, under, through etc.
(prepositions of place and direction)

170   Some customers in the supermarket can't find what they want. You are the assistant. Complete the sentences.

1 I can't find the cereals.
   YOU: They're ...*on*......... the left, ...*on*......... the bottom shelf, ..*below*.... the sugar.

2 Where's the rice, please?
   YOU: It's .... the left, ... the top shelf, ... the pasta and the bread.

3 Where are the biscuits, please?
   YOU: They're .... the right, ... shelf, ... the nuts.

4 Where's the water, please?
   YOU: It's .... the right, ... shelf, ... the cola.

5 I can't find the tea.
   YOU: It's .... the right, ... shelf, ... the cola.

6 And the cakes?
   YOU: They're .... the cola, ... shelf, ... middle, ... the
        biscuits and the chocolate.

Now you say where the coffee is.

7 The coffee is ....

And the flour?

8 The flour is ....

171 Look at John's travel plans for September. Complete his story using **to/in/at** if necessary. In one sentence no preposition is necessary.

Sunday 2nd	Flight London → Rome, Italy (arrive Rome airport 11.00) (Park Hotel)
Wednesday 5th	Flight Rome → Bangkok, Thailand (Plaza Hotel)
Monday 10th	Boat Bangkok → Ko Samui
Wednesday 12th	Ko Samui
Wednesday 26th	Return Ko Samui → Bangkok
Friday 28th	Flight Bangkok → London
Saturday 29th	Arrive London Heathrow

I'm flying (1) _to_ Italy on Sunday 2nd September, and the plane arrives (2) .... Rome airport at 11.00. I'm staying (3) .... Rome (4) .... the Park Hotel for three days. Then, on Wednesday, I'm going (5) .... Thailand for five days. I'll arrive (6) .... the Plaza Hotel (7) .... the centre of Bangkok late on Wednesday evening. On Saturday I'm meeting a friend of mine (8) .... the hotel. He lives (9) .... the north of Thailand and is coming (10) .... Bangkok. We are going on holiday together.

On Monday the 10th, we are taking a boat (11) .... one of the islands, Ko Samui. The journey takes three days so we arrive there on Wednesday evening. We're staying there for two weeks. It's going to be wonderful. On the 26th we return by boat and get back (12) .... Bangkok on the 28th. Early the next day I fly back (13) .... England. I arrive (14) .... home in the middle of the night. A wonderful month for me!

172 A visit from the neighbour's cat. Look at the journey that Felix made in Sue's garden. Complete the story with prepositions (**over / up / out of / into** etc.).

Felix jumped (1) _over_ the wall and walked (2) _across_ the grass. Then he went (3) .... the pond and (4) .... the path. He walked (5) .... Sue's chair and (6) .... the table. Suddenly he jumped (7) .... the table and took the fish which was (8) .... Sue's plate. He jumped (9) .... the table with the fish. Then the dog, Rosie, came (10) .... the house and chased the cat. They both ran (11) .... the bushes and (12) .... the patio. Felix stopped suddenly but Rosie fell (13) .... the pond. Felix looked at her and then jumped (14) .... the wall again, still holding the fish.

prepositions (general)

173 Read sentence (a) and then write sentence (b). Use the word in brackets ( ) + a preposition (**to/at/with** etc.).

1 a) I always got the best mark in History at school.
   b) I _was good at History at school._ (good)

2 a) The apples you bought yesterday were green. These are red.
   b) These apples .... (different)

3 a) Turn the TV off, please. It's football and I don't like it.
   b) I .... (not interested)

4 a) This is Kate's husband, Carl.
   b) Kate .... (married)

5 a) Rain, rain, rain! I'd like some sunshine for a change.
   b) I .... (fed up)

6 a) Jim doesn't like storms. They frighten him.
   b) Jim .... (afraid)

7 a) Stuart can't cook. A boiled egg is too difficult for him!
   b) Stuart .... (not very good)

8 a) Oliver always does the shopping for his elderly neighbours.
   b) Oliver .... (nice)

9 a) You can't move in my grandmother's sitting room. She's got a lot of furniture.
   b) My grandmother's sitting room .... (full)

10 a) Why are you shouting at Liz?
   b) Why ....? (angry)

174 Put in a preposition (**of/to/for** etc.) where necessary.

1 It was really nice _of_ Lisa to send you a birthday present. You must write _to_ her and thank her .... it.

2 If you've got a problem, you can always talk .... Janet .... it. She's very good .... listening .... people.

3 A: What's happened .... you? You look very wet.
   B: I was fed up .... waiting .... a bus so I walked home, but then it started raining.

4 I must remember to telephone .... Sarah tonight. I want to ask her .... some information about hotels in Madrid. I'm thinking .... going there in the autumn.

5 A: Have you got any books .... Luke Allen? Do you think I'll like his writing?
   B: It depends .... what kind of stories you like. This one, for example, is .... his time in prison.

6 We're going .... holiday on Saturday. Could you look .... the cat for us?

7 A: Martha spent two hours .... the phone last night, talking .... her boyfriend.
   B: What were they talking ....?
   A: I don't know, but she was very nice .... him.

8 A: Does this pen belong .... anyone here?
   B: Yes, me. I've been looking .... it for ages.

9 We didn't have to wait .... the train. It arrived .... time.

175   Complete the sentences. Use a preposition + the verb in brackets ( ).

> *Dear Lynn*
>
> *Thank you* (1) *for sending* ..... *(send) me the photos of John. I'm*
> *sorry* (2) .... *(not / write) before but I've been very busy. My job*
> *is taking a lot of my time at the moment. In fact, I'm thinking*
> (3) .... *(leave). I'm not really interested* (4) .... *(sell)*
> *cars any more. I liked the job at first but now I'm fed up* (5) ....
> *(say) the same things to everyone – you know, how wonderful the cars*
> *are, etc. Do you think I should look for a new job? It's a big decision to*
> *take. I'm a bit afraid* (6) .... *(be) unemployed. I know I'm*
> *good* (7) .... *(sell) things but the employment situation is*
> *difficult at the moment. What's your advice?*
>
> *Hope to hear from you soon.*
> *Love Mark*

go in, put on etc. (phrasal verbs)

176   Complete the sentences with you **up/off/in** etc.

1   Hurry ..up.., Pam! The plane takes ..off.. in ten minutes.
2   Jane was asleep on the bus. Suddenly, the bus driver said, 'Wake ....! This is your stop.'
    Jane quickly got .... and the bus drove ....
3   A young boy ran out of the sweet shop and rode .... on his bike. Two seconds later, the
    shop keeper came out and shouted, 'Come ....! You haven't paid!'
4   Look ....! There's an old woman trying to cross the road. I think you're driving too fast.
    Slow .... a bit, please.
5   If you've finished Exercise 6, turn .... and carry .... Exercises 7 and 8 are on page 5.
6   A: Can I speak to Bob, please?
    B: I'm sorry, I can't hear you. Can you speak ....?
    A: Can I speak to Bob, please?
    B: Yes, hold .... a minute. He's in the kitchen, washing .... I'll call him. BOB!
7   One cold night last winter my car broke .... I went to a house and asked for help. The
    man there was very kind and said, 'Come .... and keep warm.'

177   Complete the sentences with a verb + **on/off/up** etc.

1   You're in a clothes shop. You want to buy some jeans but first you want to see if they're the
    right size. What do you ask the shop assistant?
    Can I try these jeans on, please?

2   It's dark in the room. You need some light. What do you ask?
    Could you ...., please?

3   Your father can't read the newspaper because he isn't wearing his glasses.
    What do you tell him to do?
    ...., Dad.

4   You borrow some money from a friend. You promise to return it tomorrow.
    What do you say?
    I'll .... tomorrow.

5   Your grandmother has dropped a magazine on the floor and she can't get it.
    What does she ask you?
    Could you .... for me, please?

6   Your sister is playing her stereo very loudly. You don't mind, but you don't want it so loud.
    What do you ask her?
    Could you .... a bit, please?

7   You are in the sitting room and the TV is on. Your mother comes in and asks if you are
    watching it. What do you say?
    No, not really. You can ....

8   You've found some very old and very soft tomatoes in the fridge. What do you ask?
    Do you want these tomatoes or shall I ....?

when and if

178 Complete the sentences in your own words.

1   Please don't talk to me when I'm *trying to work.*
2   When John finishes university, he ....
3   My grandfather started work at the age of 14 and stopped when he ....
4   Sarah will probably buy a car when she ....
5   When you ...., you'll be surprised how much he's changed.
6   I'll give Stephanie your letter when ....
7   When I first heard the news, ...
8   I'm a bit shy when ....

179 Jill and Sue are waiting at the bus-stop. They are on their way to the cinema. Complete their story.
Use the end of the previous sentence to make the beginning of the next sentence.

Oh dear, the bus is late.
1   If the bus *doesn't arrive* soon, we'll be late.
2   If .... late, we'll miss the beginning of the film.
3   If .... the film, we won't
    understand the story.
4   If .... the story, we'll be bored.
5   If ...., we'll probably fall asleep.
6   If ...., we'll miss the end of the film.
    Let's not go to the cinema.

180   Look at the two underlined parts of these sentences. One part is right and the other is wrong. Correct the wrong part.

1 When <u>you come</u> home tonight, <u>we go</u> and see Fred in hospital.   .... *we will go* ....
2 <u>I'm going to</u> visit the Colosseum when <u>I'll be</u> in Rome. ....
3 <u>Do you tell</u> me what happened when <u>I see</u> you later? ....
4 It's a pity this room is so small. If <u>it were</u> bigger, we <u>can put</u> all our furniture in it. ....
5 If <u>I will see</u> Ann, <u>I won't ask</u> her about her exam. ....
6 Sam doesn't get up early enough to catch the 7.30 train. If <u>he would get up</u> earlier, <u>he wouldn't be</u> late. ....
7 I'm sure Bill <u>will ring</u> you before <u>he will go</u> on holiday. ....
8 If <u>it won't rain</u> soon, all the plants <u>will die</u> in the garden. ....
9 I haven't got a bike, I'm afraid. If <u>I have</u> one, <u>I would lend</u> it to you. ....
10 Barbara is in bed with a fever. <u>She would be</u> here with us if <u>she wouldn't be</u> ill. ....

181   What do you say in the following situations? Use the words in brackets ( ) to help you.

1 Paul has asked you to go to a jazz concert. You don't like jazz so you're not going with him.
(I / go / with you / if I / like / jazz)   *I would go with you if I liked jazz.*

2 You haven't decided what to do this weekend. Perhaps you will go to London or perhaps you will stay at home and invite your boss for dinner.
(If I / not / go / to London / I / invite / my boss for dinner)
If I don't go to London, I'll invite my boss for dinner.

3 You want to go on holiday but you're very busy at work at the moment.
(If I / not / be / busy at work / I / go / on holiday)
....

4 You're in a restaurant with your sister. She's got some onions on her plate. You know she doesn't like them but you do!
(I / eat your onions / if you / not / want them)
....

5 You want to buy a new computer. The one you are looking at is quite cheap but it doesn't have a very big memory.
(If it / have / a bigger memory / I / buy / it)
....

6 You and Clare are outside the cinema, waiting for David. He's late and the film starts in five minutes.
(We / miss the beginning / if he / not / arrive / soon)
....

7 Your brother is going to buy an old car in bad condition. You don't think it's a good idea.
(I / not / buy it / if I / be / you)
....

8 I don't have any money because I don't have a job.
(If I / have / a job / I / have / some money)
....

the person who ... / the people we met (relative clauses)

Units 113–114

182 Make one sentence from two sentences. Use **who** or **which**.

1 James lives on an island. It's famous for its beautiful beaches.
   James _lives on an island which is famous for its beautiful beaches._

2 There's a new chef in our canteen. He's very good at making desserts.
   There's a new chef ....

3 A car crashed into mine. It was green.
   The car ....

4 Where's the newspaper? It was on the table.
   Where ....?

5 A handbag was left on the bus yesterday. It belongs to my sister.
   The handbag .... my sister.

6 I spoke to an assistant. She had long, dark hair.
   I ....

7 Peter writes books. They are translated into many languages.
   Peter ....

8 A lot of people went to last night's concert. They enjoyed it.
   The people ....

183 Make one sentence from two sentences.

1 Jill is looking at a man. She thinks she knows him.
   Jill thinks she knows _the man she's looking at._

2 Sally stayed with some friends. What's their name?
   What's the name ....?

3 I worked in a shop. It was called 'Bangles'.
   The shop I ....

4 I was talking to some people. They're friends of your father's.
   The people I ....

5 You were looking for a woman. Did you find her?
   Did you find the ....?

6 Kate went on holiday with some people. They lived in the same street.
   The people ....

7 I'm listening to some music. It was written over 300 years ago.
   The music ....

8 Fiona's playing tennis with a man. Who is he?
   Who's the ....?

184 Complete the sentences. Use the information in brackets.

GUIDE: Ladies and gentlemen, this is the house (1) __Michael Barnes was born in.__
            (*Michael Barnes was born in this house.*)

CLARE: Who's Michael Barnes?

ADAM: He's the man (2) ....
            (*Michael Barnes wrote over 100 books.*)

CLARE: I've never heard of him.

ADAM: You have! You know that film (3) .... ?
            (*We went to see a film last week.*) Well it was based on one of his books.

CLARE: Oh.

GUIDE: And now, if you look on your right you can see Jane Carter's house.

CLARE: Why is that important?

ADAM: You must remember! Jane Carter is the woman (4) ....
            (*I told you about Jane Carter.*)

CLARE: Oh yes. She lived until she was over a hundred.

ADAM: That's right. And do you remember the name of the institute (5) ....
            .... (*The institute was founded by Jane Carter.*)

CLARE: The Fellcome Institute, wasn't it?

ADAM: Yes, and if you remember, it was the Fellcome Institute (6) ....
            ....

            (*The Fellcome Institute was closed down by the authorities in the 1950s.*)

CLARE: I remember now. So this is her house. Interesting.

GUIDE: And now, let's go into the main street and look at …